MW00581129

30-DAY
KeyboardWorkout

An Exercise Plan for Keyboardists

Tom Brislin

Alfred Music
P.O. Box 10003
Van Nuys, CA 91410-0003
alfred.com

Copyright © MCMXCIX by Alfred Music
All rights reserved

ISBN-10: 0-7390-0230-9
ISBN-13: 978-0-7390-0230-8

Cover Art: Photodisc, photograph of man playing keyboards by Karen Miller

Contents

About the Author

Tom Brislin is a keyboardist, vocalist and songwriter who appears regularly in the New York and New Jersey areas. He has performed and/or recorded with artists in many styles of music, including Meat Loaf, Glen Burtnik and Michael Brecker. Currently, he fronts the original modern-rock band, You Were Spiraling, and has produced the band's two independently-released CDs: "You Were Spiraling" (1994) and "The Hello CD" (1997). Tom has also been active in the jazz scene, performing with various jazz groups. A piano instructor, he has worked with students privately as well as at the Jazz Studies Department of William Paterson University, of which he is a graduate.

Acknowledgements

I'd like to thank the following people for their support, wisdom and/or coaching: the Brislin family, Anita DeSorbo, Gary Kirkpatrick, David Demsey, Rufus Reid, Harold Mabern, Norman Simmons, Pete Malinverni, Vinson Hill, Sister Delores Margaret, Dan Schultz, J.R. Thompson, Noah Baerman, Jody Fisher, Damon La Scot and Michael Kahn.

Introduction

Many keyboardists start off their daily practice routine with exercises. The piano, organ and other keyboard instruments pose numerous physical demands. Over the years, many great keyboard technique texts have been written to help give players the strength and dexterity necessary to meet those demands. This book offers a fun collection of new and classic exercises and, most importantly, *a plan*. This plan will help you get into a daily practice routine yet is flexible enough to be used in different ways for different players.

There are several ways you can use this book:

1. Learn the warm-ups and go through the first 30-day workout as prescribed.
2. Learn the warm-ups and go through the second, extended 30-day workout as prescribed.
3. Learn the warm-ups and go through *both* 30-day workouts.
4. Look for exercises that target specific problems you may have.
5. Work only on the chord exercises.
6. Work only on the single-note line exercises.
7. Learn the scales and chords in the appendix and play the chord exercises as prescribed.
8. Just learn and play the warm-ups.

Begin by doing the warm-up exercises for a few days. This will give you enough "chops" to dig into the Workouts.

Next, we venture into the Workouts. The first time around, you should spend a few days learning each Workout. Gain an understanding of what's going on, and make sure you're playing the exercise smoothly before moving on to the next one.

Once you've completed the first plan, it will be easier to judge how much time you'll need for your own workout. Some exercises will require more time than others. Don't be afraid to create your own variations on what is presented here. It won't take long to learn, but gaining precision is a lifelong job. If specific areas are causing you consistent trouble, zero in on them and *work them out!*

You will notice that specific tempo and dynamic markings are not provided. It is the nature of these warm ups and workouts that these elements will vary. Sometimes, specific dynamics, or even articulations, are suggested as variations. You should learn every exercise slowly at first, and then develop your ability to play it at faster tempos. Make sure that dynamics and tempo are always a part of your thinking as you experiment with each exercise.

> *DO NOT SPEND ALL YOUR TIME ON THIS WORK!*
> It's great to gain strength and dexterity on your instrument—but remember what those chops are used for: *playing music.* Devote most of your time to learning new music, reviewing the old and even creating some of your own. Periodically, focus on technique for an extended amount of time. Get into the "woodshed" and bring this book with you. Have fun!

Section One Terms, Geography and Reading Music

Let's review some basic musical terms we'll come across in the workouts.

The Keyboard

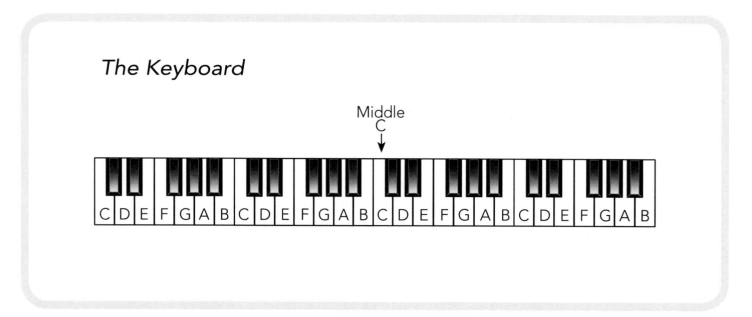

Pitches on the Grand Staff

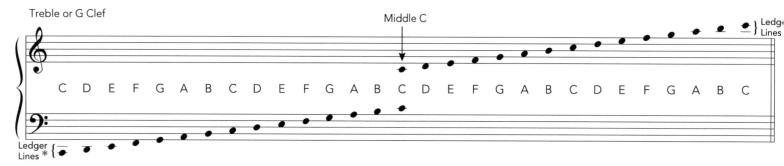

* Ledger lines are short horizontal lines used to extend the staff either higher or lower.

Finger Numbers

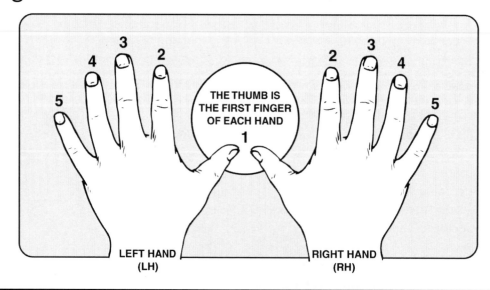

Measures and Bar Lines

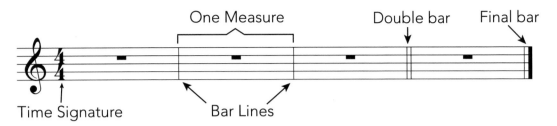

One Measure   Double bar   Final bar

Time Signature   Bar Lines

Note and Rest Values

𝅝	𝅗𝅥 𝅗𝅥	♩ ♩	♪ ♪	𝅘𝅥𝅯 𝅘𝅥𝅯
Whole note 4 beats	Half notes 2 beats each	Quarter notes 1 beat each	Eighth notes ½ beat each	Sixteenth notes ¼ beat each
𝄻	𝄼	𝄽	𝄾	𝄿
Whole note rest 4 beats	Half note rest 2 beats	Quarter note rest 1 beat	Eighth note rest ½ beat	Sixteenth note rest ¼ beat

Time Signatures

The top number indicates how many beats are in each measure. The bottom number indicates what kind of note gets one count.

$\frac{4}{4}$ 4 beats per measure $\frac{3}{4}$ 3 beats per measure
    Quarter note ♩ = 1 beat   Quarter note ♩ = 1 beat

Sometimes a 𝄴 is used in place of a numerical time signature. This stands for common time which is another way of expressing $\frac{4}{4}$ time, the most commonly used time signature.

Miscellaneous

♯   *Sharp.* When placed before a note, it means to play the note one half step higher (play the nearest higher pitch).

♭   *Flat.* When placed before a note, it means to play the note one half step lower (play the nearest lower pitch).

♮   *Natural.* When placed before a note already sharp or flat, return to the natural note (white key).

8*va*   *Ottava alta.* When placed above the music, all notes under the bracket should be played one octave higher. When placed below the music, all notes above the bracket should be played one octave lower.

⌢   *Fermata.* When placed over a note, hold a little bit longer than its normal duration.

Roman Numerals
Shown with their Arabic equivalents

I ....i 1	III....iii ...3	V .....v....5	VII... vii... 7
II .....ii ... 2	IV.... iv...4	VI....vi... 6	

Section Two

Warming the Hands

Try running warm water over your hands for a few minutes each time before you play. This will get the blood flowing in the hands and will help you ease into a good workout. This is also useful right before a performance when there is no keyboard available to warm-up on.

Stretching

Athletes, and those who exercise frequently, know the importance of stretching before they engage in a repetitive activity. As musicians, we would be wise to do the same. A word of advice: When you stretch, you should do so simply and gently. You can get a good stretch by simply raising the arms upward and out (don't bend your elbows). While in this position, bend at the wrist so your fingers point up, as if giving someone the signal to "stop." Slowly move the hand down in the same manner. Keep it gentle. Your best bet is to consult a qualified health professional for more information about stretching techniques.

Breathing

Don't forget to breathe! As obvious as it sounds, it's easy to forget to breathe regularly when the brain is busy making sure that the fingers are doing exactly what they're supposed to do. Good breathing helps you relax and therefore helps your technique become smoother.

Listening

Like breathing, an obviously important yet often overlooked activity is listening as you play. Sure, exercises may not be as fun to listen to as your favorite pieces, but it is important to pay close attention to the sound you are getting from your instrument. Are you playing in the correct rhythm? Are you observing dynamics? Are you playing with clarity?

Signals from Your Body

Pay attention to the signals you get from your body. If you experience pain in your hands, wrists or arms at any point during your workout, stop! That's a message telling you something isn't right. Don't be a hero. Your chops will come if you practice consistently and increase your workload gradually. Repetitive strain injuries are easy to get and hard to recover from. Be careful.

Posture

The Body

You've heard it a thousand times before, and here comes a thousand and one: sit up straight! You can lean forward slightly at times, which can be useful for digging into some meaty chords, etc. When sitting at the piano or keyboard, your arms should be parallel with the floor and level with the keys. Adjust the height of your bench to attain this position. If your bench isn't adjustable, try one of these solutions:

1. If it's too low, try using a pillow or a trusty old phone book to raise your position.
2. If the bench is too high, try sitting a little farther away from the keys.

The Hands

Once you are in a good playing position, your hands should rest on top of the keys. Let the fingers curve slightly. Keep the wrists from falling but don't tense up. As you play, it's good to have some flexibility with the wrists but make sure they aren't below the level of the keys. Otherwise, the fingers would have to reach up above the keys before pressing them down. That's extra work that we want to avoid.

Section Three Warm-Up Exercises

We're about ready to dig into the workout. However, just as an athlete must warm-up their muscles before strenuous activity, we should do some warm-up exercises at the keyboard. You'll find that this warm-up routine gets the blood flowing in the hands, even (and especially) when you play the exercises slowly.

There are four separate warm-up exercises. Numbers 1, 2 and 4 deal primarily with finger independence while number 3 works the forearms and hands.

Warm-Up Exercise #1
Independent Digits

Play this exercise slowly. Lightly press down and hold all five fingers of each hand on the keys for the notes shown in the first measure. Both hands play a repeating note with finger 1 while the other fingers are held down. Then hold finger 1 down with the others as you play repeated notes with finger 2, then hold finger 2 down as you play with finger 3, etc. Continue to hold all other fingers down as you play each measure. Once this is completed, you should reverse the exercise, playing all the fingers from 5 inward toward 1. Remember not to get too tense!

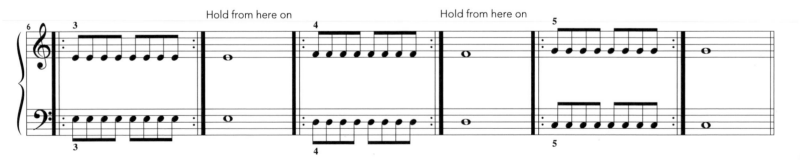

Warm-Up Exercise #2
Parallel Motion

Parallel motion is when multiple lines of music move in the same direction, ascending or descending, with the same intervals. In this warm-up, the five fingers of both hands play up and down the lower five notes of the major scale in all keys. Use the same fingering for each key.

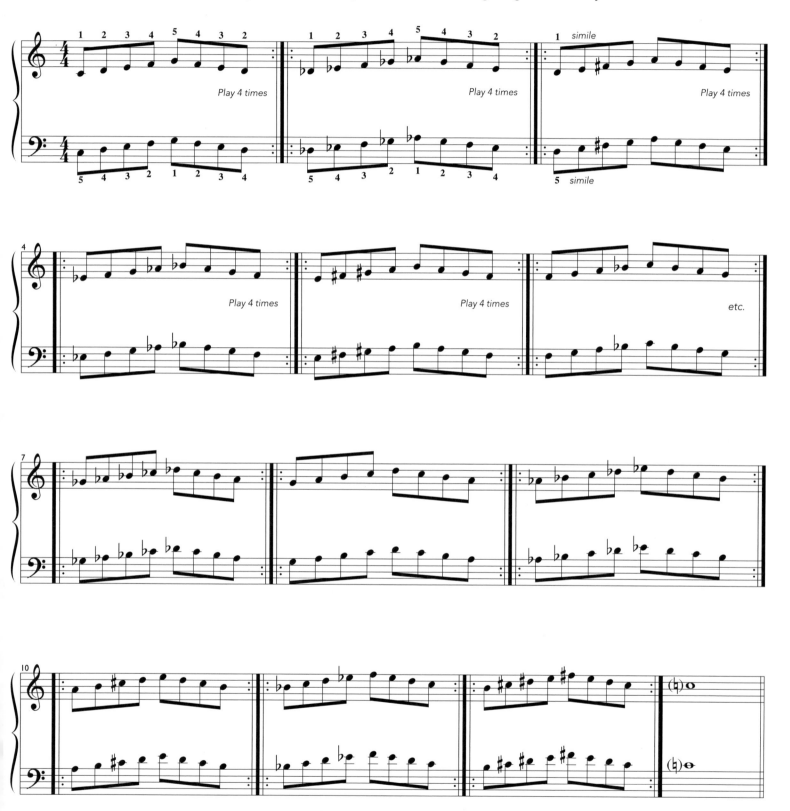

Warm-Up Exercise #3
Octave Jumps

The forearms are used often in expressive keyboard playing, so it makes sense to warm them up as well. Both hands play octaves, repeating then jumping up to the same note one octave higher. Do this over four octaves (or however many your keyboard will accommodate), then make your way down the keyboard in the same manner. Play through all twelve keys, and keep your wrists flexible without collapsing them. For a challenging variation, play slowly without looking at the keys.

Warm-Up Exercise #4
Trill-a-thon

This exercise deals with the *trill*, which is alternating two neighboring notes, often rapidly. But not so fast, partner—you should start by practicing slowly. We will cover every pair of adjacent fingers. Go for clarity and the trills will shimmer when brought up to speed.

ion Four

The Proficiency Workout

Now that we know the basic warm-ups, we can begin the Workouts. There are two groups of thirty separate Workouts. The first group is a no-nonsense approach accessible to those at the intermediate level of keyboard playing, as well as providing a good practice plan for those with a higher level of keyboard experience. We'll call the first group "The Proficiency Workout." The second group raises the bar, providing more challenging variations of the principles explored in the first group. We'll call this group "The Extended Proficiency Workout."

Each day's Workout will feature exercises called *Linear Sprints* that develop finger dexterity. Then there are exercises called *Chord-Toners*, helpful in developing technique and familiarity with chords. Variations in fingering, tempo, articulation and dynamics are provided to keep the Workouts fresh and keep you "on your toes." The Workouts will help you improve as a player and keep your technique in shape for most musical situations. Keep in mind that everyone has their own pace, and there are many challenges presented here. It's important to put in a consistent amount of time on each exercise, even if it means just a few minutes each day. There will always be time to go back and try variations that you skip the first time around. Be dedicated but be patient as well, and remember that technique is only part of the great art of music! It is no substitute for great musicianship and creativity.

Ready? Okay...

DAY ONE

Warm-Ups #1-4
Linear Sprint #1

30 DAY KEYBOARD WORKOUT						
1✔	2	3	4	5	6	7
8	9	10	11	12	13	14
15	16	17	18	19	20	21
22	23	24	25	26	27	28
29	30					

We'll start off by playing a chromatic scale with both hands two octaves apart, ascending for two octaves and then descending. Start with a slow, even tempo. Make sure you use the given fingerings and play with a smooth, legato feel. Once you get the hang of it, try to master this exercise without looking at the keys.

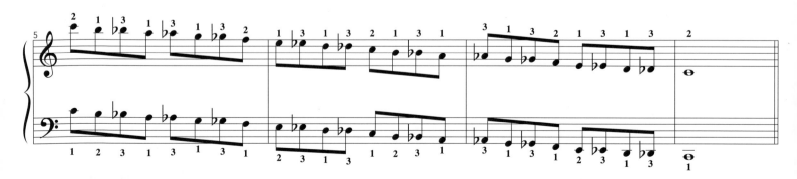

Chord-Toner #1

This exercise has a diatonic 7th chord built on each note of a C Major scale. Practice slowly so that you know what notes you're moving to before you actually play each succeeding chord. Make sure all the tones sound simultaneously, and hold the chord for the full duration before moving to the next.

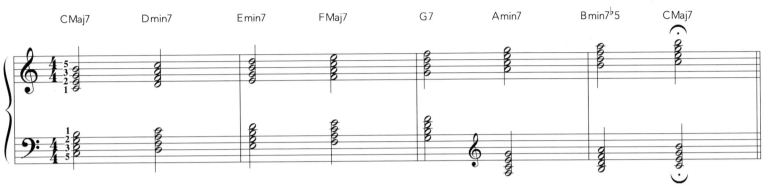

Try practicing this in other keys and if you can, in all twelve. The Appendix starting on page 87 shows all the key signatures, which will help. The sequence of chord types is the same in every major key:

I	ii	iii	IV	V	vi	vii	I
Maj7	min7	min7	Maj7	Dom7	min7	min7$\flat$5	Maj7

We'll show examples in several keys throughout these workouts. The ability to transpose a chord sequence to any key is an invaluable skill, so give it a try!

Variations:

1. Practice Linear Sprint #1 with a short, detached staccato feel. Play at a soft, consistent volume.
2. Practice Chord-Toner #1 leaving off the highest-pitched note in each chord in each hand. You are now harmonizing the scale in triads instead of 7th chords. Triads are fundamental chords found in many styles of music.

DAY TWO

30 DAY KEYBOARD WORKOUT						
✓	✓	3	4	5	6	7
8	9	10	11	12	13	14
15	16	17	18	19	20	21
22	23	24	25	26	27	28
29	30					

Warm-Ups #1-4
Linear Sprint #2

The pattern in this exercise uses the chromatic scale. Play slowly at first, paying special attention to controlling evenness of volume. Keep that control when bringing it up to speed. When memorizing the chromatic scale and its patterns, notice the finger 2 landings (circled). In the right hand, finger 2 plays C and F and, in the left hand, E and B. Both hands play all other white keys with finger 1 and black keys with finger 3.

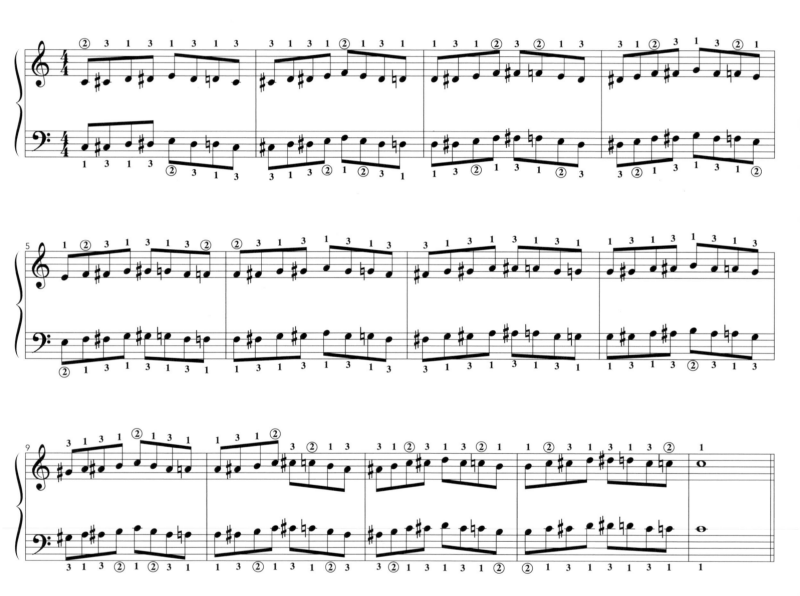

Chord-Toner #2

Memorize the harmonized scale below. These are the diatonic 7th chords in the key of F Major. Try to make a smooth transition from chord to chord, sounding all chord tones at the exact same time and holding them for two full beats each.

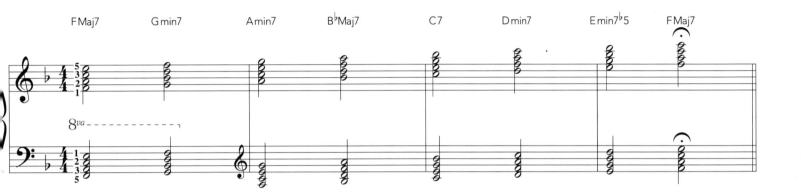

Variations:

1. Practice Linear Sprint #2 with a short, detached staccato feel. Play at a soft, consistent volume.
2. Practice Linear Sprint #2 playing each measure twice before moving on to the next.
3. Practice Chord-Toner #2 leaving off the highest-pitched note of each chord in each hand. You are now harmonizing the scale in triads instead of 7th chords.
4. Practice Chord-Toner #2 with the new position and fingering shown below. The chords are now in *first inversion*. The root of each chord is now the highest pitch, leaving the 3rd of each chord as the lowest.

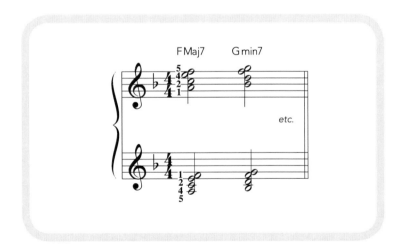

DAY THREE
Warm-Ups #1-4
Linear Sprint #3

Play the following one-measure, chromatic triplet pattern up through one octave. Start slowly, and be careful not to accent beats one and three of each measure. Keep the same evenness when bringing the exercise up in tempo. Refer to page 16 for an explanation of the fingerings.

30 DAY KEYBOARD WORKOUT						
1	2	3	4	5	6	7
8	9	10	11	12	13	14
15	16	17	18	19	20	21
22	23	24	25	26	27	28
29	30					

Chord-Toner #3

Memorize the following harmonized B♭ Major scale. Make sure all of the notes of each chord sound simultaneously and are held for the full two beats before moving to the next chord. In Chord Toners #1 - #3, you have done this in C, F and B♭. Now try it in all the other keys.

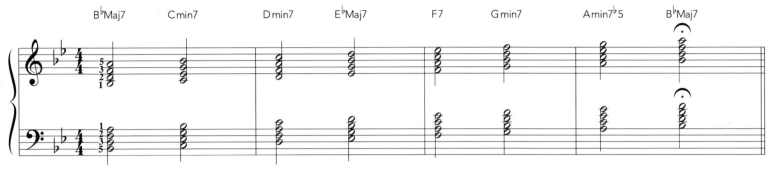

Variations:

1. Practice Linear Sprint #3 with a short, detached staccato feel. Play at a soft, consistent volume.
2. Practice Chord-Toner #3 leaving off the highest-pitched note of each chord in each hand. You are now playing triads.
3. Practice Chord-Toner #3 with the position and fingering shown below. The chords are now in first inversion. Try transposing to all keys.

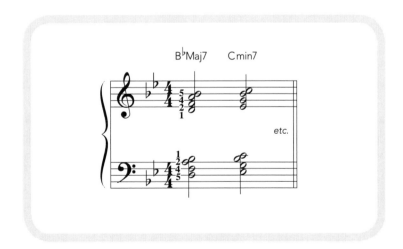

DAY FOUR
Warm-Ups #1-4
Linear Sprint #4

30 DAY KEYBOARD WORKOUT

1	2	3	4	5	6	7
8	9	10	11	12	13	14
15	16	17	18	19	20	21
22	23	24	25	26	27	28
29	30					

Below is a one-beat pattern using the chromatic scale and triplets. Notice how often finger 3 (in both hands) crosses over each side of the thumb. Make sure your wrists stay flexible without collapsing. As usual, start slowly and go for a smooth, even sound.

Chord-Toner #4

This exercise makes a pattern out of the *diatonic chords* (harmonized scale) from Chord-Toner #1. As with the other Chord-Toners, make sure all the notes in each chord sound simultaneously. Think ahead to the next chord shape before moving your hands, and make sure you are getting there in time. It's better to play slowly and stay in tempo than to miss a beat. Play this again using the chords in F Major from Day 2 (page 17) and in B♭ from Day 3 (page 19). If you can, transpose it to other keys.

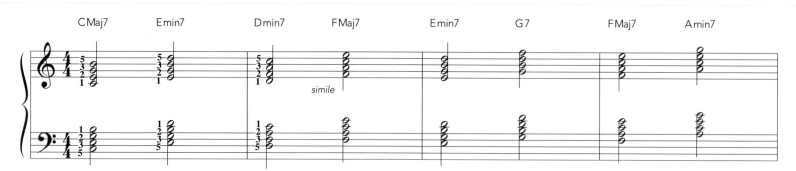

(Continued on page 21)

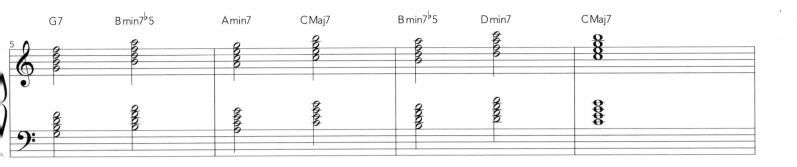

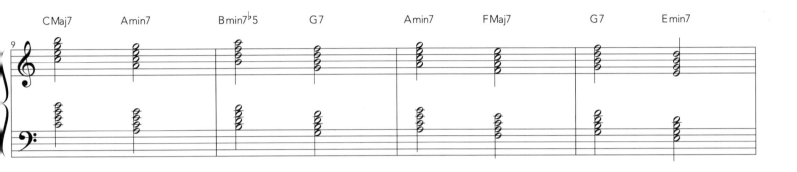

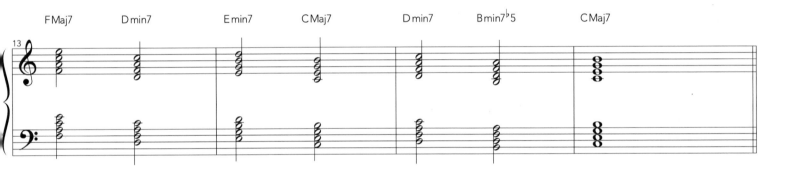

Variations:

1. Practice Linear Sprint #4 with a short, detached staccato feel. Play at a soft, consistent volume.
2. Practice Chord-Toner #4 leaving off the highest-pitched note of each chord in each hand.
3. Practice Chord-Toner #4 with the chords in first inversion. The position and fingering is shown below. Try this exercise in all keys.

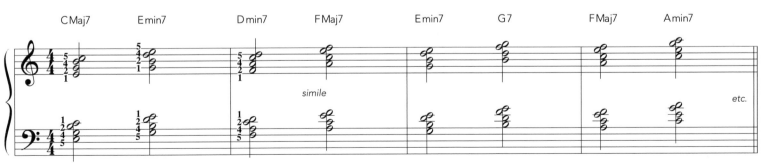

DAY FIVE

Warm-Ups #1-4
Linear Sprint #5

30 DAY KEYBOARD WORKOUT

1	2	3	4	5	6	7
8	9	10	11	12	13	14
15	16	17	18	19	20	21
22	23	24	25	26	27	28
29	30					

In all the Linear Sprints so far, we've been sticking to the chromatic scale, which is made up of *half steps* (the smallest distance between two notes). Today's Linear Sprint uses a pattern of *whole steps* (a distance equal to two half steps) moving up chromatically through one octave. Also new in this Linear Sprint is the use of finger 4. Pay strict attention to the fingerings and when you're comfortable with this exercise, play it up and down through two octaves.

Chord-Toner #5

The chord pattern below uses the diatonic 7th chords for F Major from Day Two (page 17). There's a wider jump from chord to chord, so remember to "look before you leap." Try this using the chords from Day One (page 15) and Day Three (page 19). Eventually, you will become confident about where the shapes lie on the keyboard, and will be able to play chord patterns like these without having to look at the keys.

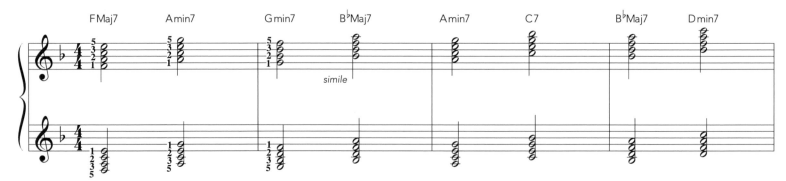

(Continued on page 23)

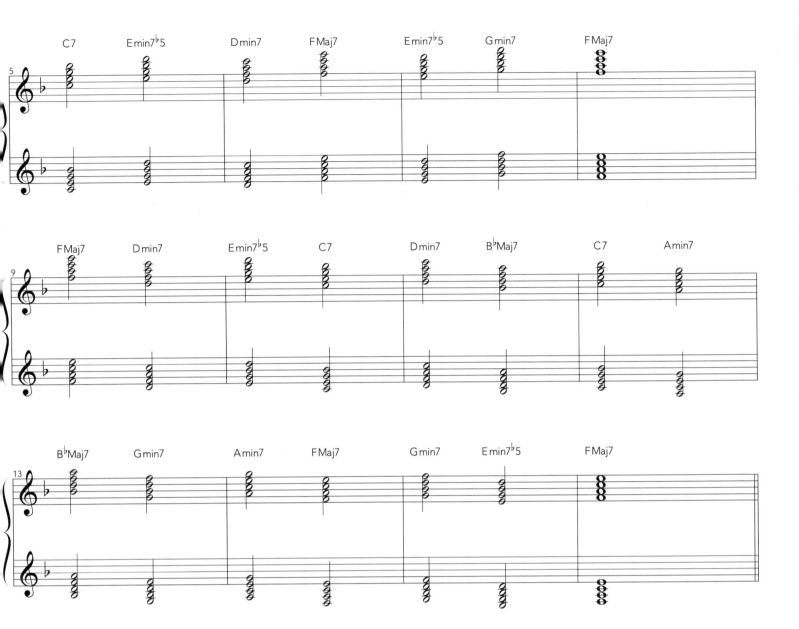

Variations:

1. Practice Linear Sprint #5 with a short, detached staccato feel. Play at a soft, consistent volume.
2. Practice Chord-Toner #5 leaving off the highest-pitched note of each chord in each hand, yielding the diatonic triads.
3. Play Chord-Toner #5 with the chords in first inversion. Try it in all keys.

Warm-Ups #1-4
Linear Sprint #6

30 DAY KEYBOARD WORKOUT

1	2	3	4	5	6	7
✓	✓	✓	✓	✓	✓	
8	9	10	11	12	13	14
15	16	17	18	19	20	21
22	23	24	25	26	27	28
29	30					

Now that you've been playing Linear Sprints using both half steps and whole steps, we'll move on to an exercise based on the major scale, which includes both. Instead of going straight up and down the scale, however, today's Linear Sprint pattern uses the scale in a slightly different way. It starts with the *tonic* (first tone), moves up one step and descends back. Then the scale moves up to the third degree, then descends back home to the tonic. It then continues up to the fourth degree, descends, goes up to the fifth degree, descends, etc. By the end of the exercise, you'll have completed the scale. Try it in all keys. All major scales and their fingerings can be found in the Appendix starting on page 87.

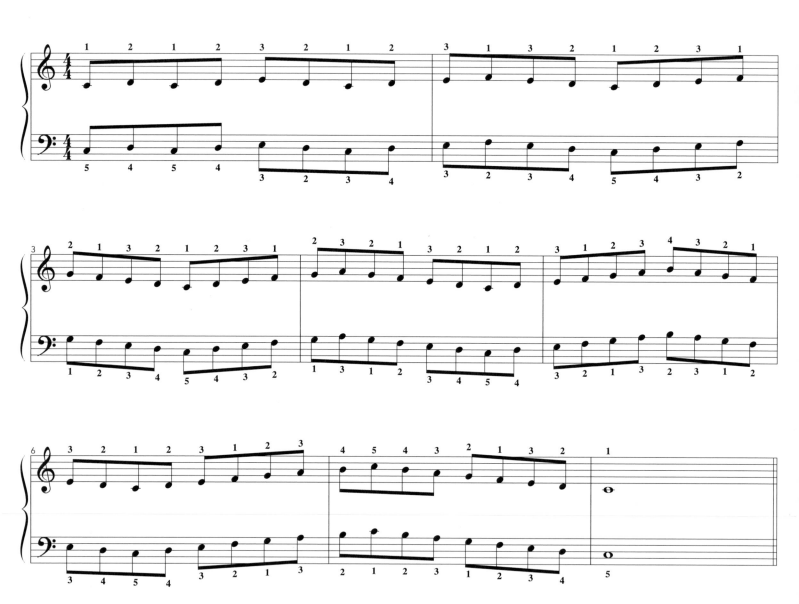

Chord-Toner #6

This chord pattern uses the diatonic 7th chords in B♭ Major from Day Three (page 19). Play this using the chords from Day One (page 15) and Day Two (page 17). The chords move in *steps* (whole steps and half steps) as well as *skips* (larger intervals—in this case, 3rds). Try playing it without looking at the keys. Try transposing it to other keys, too.

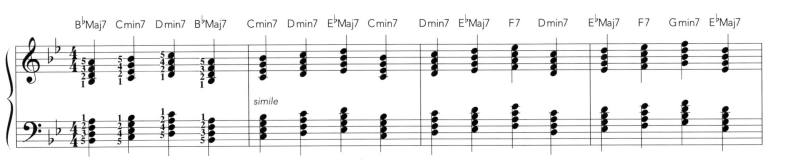

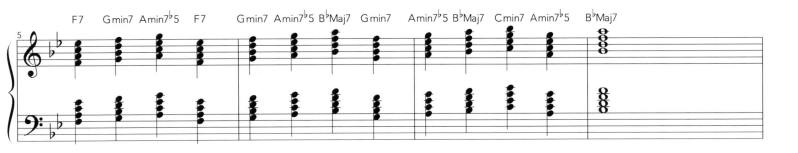

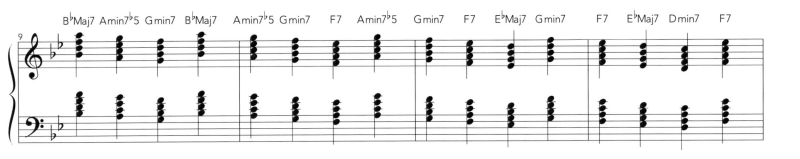

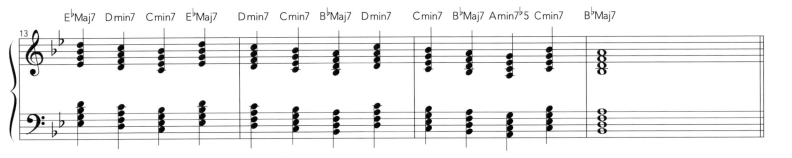

Variations:

1. Practice Linear Sprint #6 with a short, detached staccato feel. Play at a soft, consistent volume.
2. Practice Chord-Toner #6 leaving off the highest-pitched note of each chord in each hand, yielding the diatonic triads.
3. Play Chord-Toner #6 with the chords in first inversion. Try it in all keys.

DAY SEVEN

Warm-Ups #1-4
Linear Sprint #7

30 DAY KEYBOARD WORKOUT

1	2	3	4	5	6	7
✓	✓	✓	✓	✓	✓	✓
8	9	10	11	12	13	14
15	16	17	18	19	20	21
22	23	24	25	26	27	28
29	30					

The next three Linear Sprints are based on exercises by Charles-Louis Hanon. The patterns move within the major scale and include skips as well as steps. Remember to strive for evenness. If you've worked on exercises like these before, check out the variations listed on page 27.

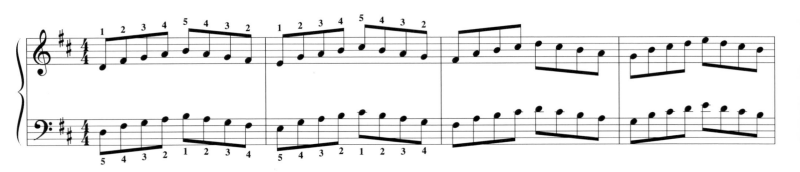

Chord-Toner #7

This exercise uses the diatonic 7th chords in the key of G Major. Each measure starts with the chord *blocked* (all the notes in the chord are played simultaneously) and ends with the same chord *arpeggiated* (broken). Lift from the forearms when playing the block chords, making sure that the attack and release of all chord-tones are synchronized.

Variations:

1. Practice Linear Sprint #7 with a short, detached staccato feel. Play at a soft, consistent volume.
2. Play the pattern in the first measure of Linear Sprint #7, then move up chromatically. Play up through one octave. Then play the pattern in the ninth measure and move down in the same chromatic manner.
3. Practice Chord-Toner #7 leaving off the highest-pitched note in each hand, yielding the diatonic triads.
4. Play Chord-Toner #7 with the chords in first inversion. Try it in all keys.

DAY EIGHT

Warm-Ups #1-4
Linear Sprint #8

30 DAY KEYBOARD WORKOUT

1	2	3	4	5	6	7
8	9	10	11	12	13	14
15	16	17	18	19	20	21
22	23	24	25	26	27	28
29	30					

Below is another exercise based on the works of Hanon. Again, the pattern moves within the major scale, this time in the key of A Major. Once you are comfortable with the Linear Sprint in this key, try it in C Major, G Major, D Major and in as many other keys as you can. Notice that the pattern includes the interval of a 4th (from the second to the third note in the pattern), which is a slightly wider skip. Stay in control!

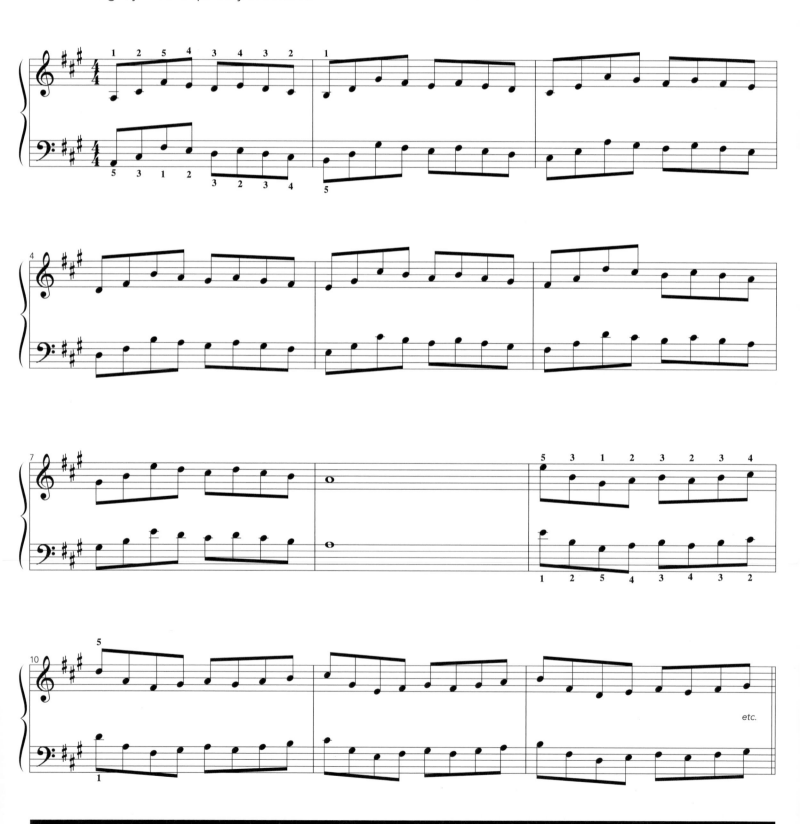

Chord-Toner #8

This four-chord pattern uses the diatonic 7th chords in the key of D Major. The pattern of the root movement of the chords is as follows: up a 5th, up to the octave and back down to the starting chord. Then the pattern repeats starting one step higher. On the way back down, the pattern starts at the higher octave, moves down a 4th, down to the lower octave and then back up to the starting chord. Then the pattern repeats one step lower. Play this using the chords from Day One (page 15), Day Two (page 17) and Day Three (page 19). Also, try moving to other keys and see how you do without looking at the keyboard.

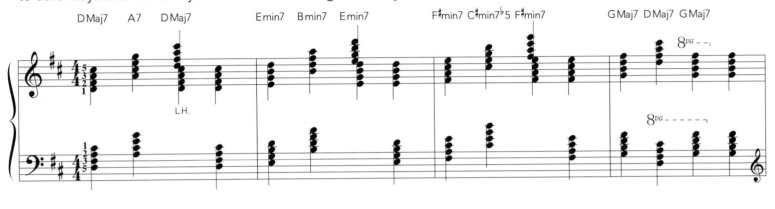

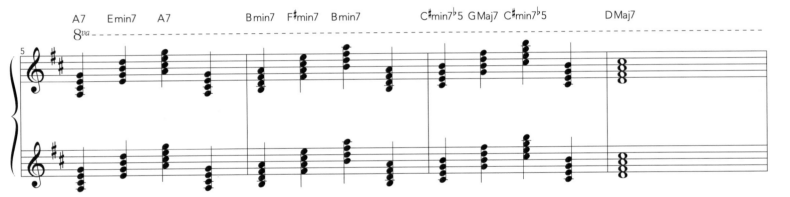

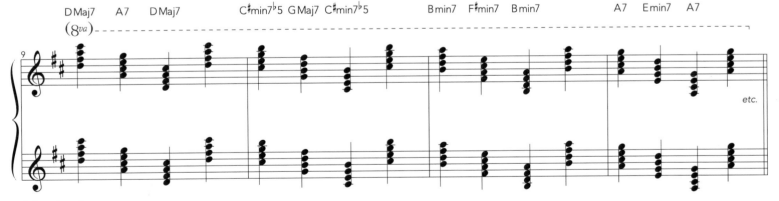

Variations:

1. Practice Linear Sprint #8 with a short, detached staccato feel. Play at a soft, consistent volume.
2. Play the pattern in the first measure of Linear Sprint #8, then move up *chromatically*. Play up one octave. Then play the pattern in the ninth measure, and move down in the same chromatic manner.
3. Practice Chord-Toner #8 leaving off the highest-pitched note of each chord in each hand, yielding the diatonic triads.
4. Play Chord-Toner #8 with the chords in first inversion. Try it in all keys.

DAY NINE

Warm-Ups #1-4
Linear Sprint #9

30 DAY KEYBOARD WORKOUT

1	2	3	4	5	6	7
✓	✓	✓	✓	✓	✓	✓
8	9	10	11	12	13	14
✓	✓					
15	16	17	18	19	20	21
22	23	24	25	26	27	28
29	30					

Third in the trilogy of Hanon-esque patterns, today's Linear Sprint is shown below in the key of E Major. In one measure alone, this pattern includes 2nds, 3rds, 4ths, 5ths and 6ths. As you play the pattern, you may notice the natural tendency of your hands to rock from side to side, almost as if they were turning doorknobs. This is fine, as it is a reminder not to tense up, but make sure the notes sound even! You should also try the exercise keeping the palms face down and giving the individual fingers an extra lift. Try it in all keys.

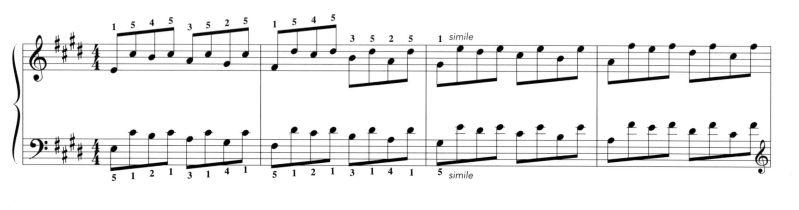

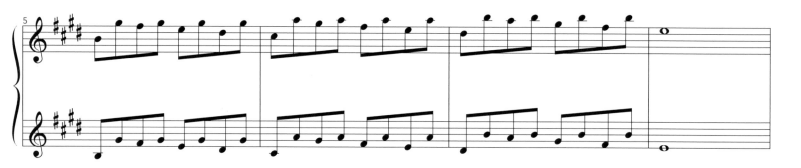

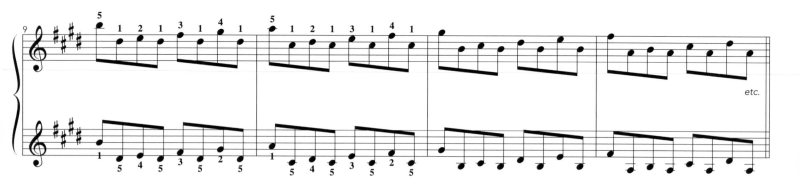

Chord-Toner #9

This chord pattern uses the diatonic 7th chords in the key of E Major. The pattern is as follows: I chord, the I chord up an octave, up a step to the ii chord, ii chord down an octave, up a step to the iii chord, iii chord up an octave, etc. Try it in all keys.

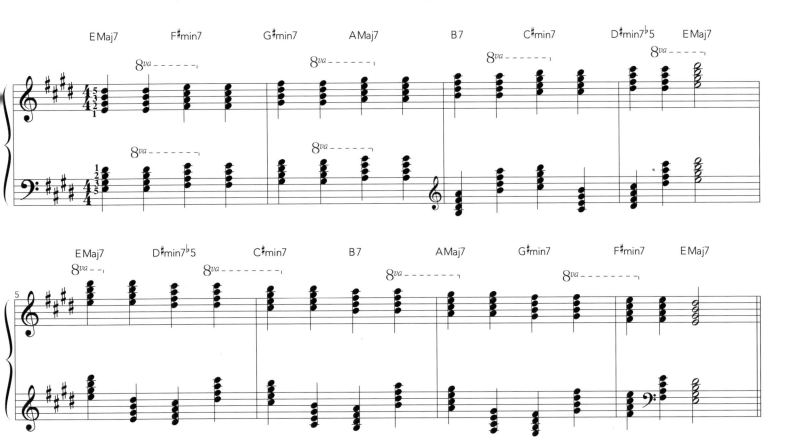

Variations:

1. Practice Linear Sprint #9 with a short, detached staccato feel. Play at a soft, consistent volume.
2. Play the pattern in the first measure of Linear Sprint #9, then move up chromatically. Play up through one octave. Then play the pattern in the ninth measure, and move down in the same chromatic manner.
3. Practice Chord-Toner #9 leaving off the highest-pitched note of each chord in each hand, yielding the diatonic triads.
4. Play Chord-Toner #9 with the chords in first inversion. Try it in all keys.

DAY TEN
Warm-Ups #1-4
Review

Today is the first review day. Practice the nine Linear Sprints you have learned thus far. Try all the variations listed, and try some new variations of your own, such as different tempos or dynamic levels.

DAY ELEVEN
Warm-Ups #1-4
Review

Today is the second review day. Now practice each Chord-Toner from the first nine days. Try playing them in all keys and with the variations. Try some new dynamic levels.

DAY TWELVE
Warm-Ups #1-4
Linear Sprint #10

Today's Linear Sprint is based on broken major triads. Start with a C Major arpeggio, move up a perfect 4th (5 half steps) and arpeggiate F Major, move up a perfect 4th and arpeggiate B♭ Major and continue in this manner (through the *cycle of 4ths*) until you arrive back at C. Stay alert, since you'll be moving around the keyboard a bit more here. Stay in control.

Chord-Toner #10

Today's Chord-Toner starts with a Cmin7♭5 chord, also known as a *half-diminished* chord. It then moves to a min7 (minor 7) chord, a 7th (dominant 7) chord and a Maj7 (major 7) chord. Notice how the hands "open up" as you move through the chord sequence. Play the same sequence up chromatically through all twelve keys. Remember to sound all chord tones simultaneously.

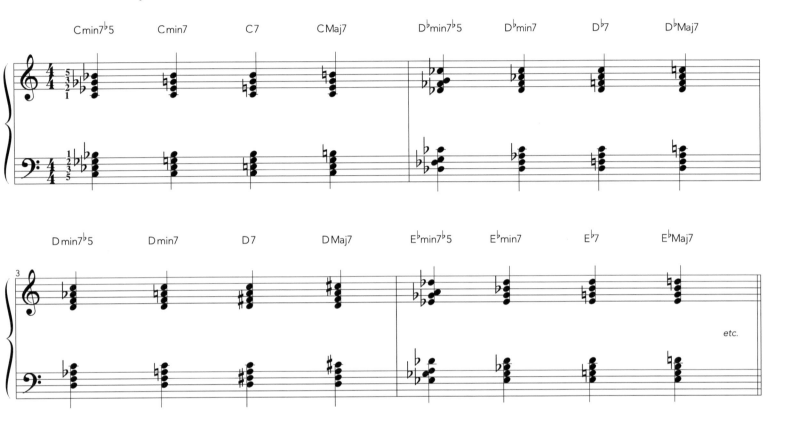

Variations:

1. Practice Linear Sprint #10 with a short, detached staccato feel. Play at a soft, consistent volume.
2. Practice Linear Sprint #10 with the hands two octaves apart.
3. Practice Chord-Toner #10 with the chords *arpeggiated* (broken) instead of blocked. Play slow eighth notes, starting at the lowest note, and play upward through the chord. The chords will change every two beats.
4. Play Chord-Toner #10 with the chords in first inversion.

DAY THIRTEEN
Warm-Ups #1-4
Linear Sprint #11

Here's another arpeggio pattern through the cycle of 4ths. This time, they are all four-note dominant 7 chords. The pattern from Day Twelve is still present but the fingering is slightly different to accommodate the extra note in each chord. As you play the highest note in each chord, move finger 1 (right hand) and finger 5 (left hand) towards the next note to make a seamless transition to the next voicing. Continue the cycle of 4ths back to C.

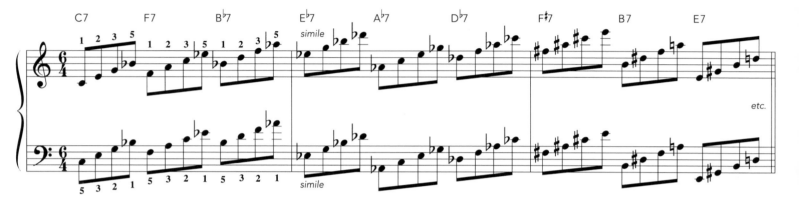

Chord-Toner #11

As in today's Linear Sprint, this Chord-Toner is based on dominant 7 chords through the cycle of 4ths. Unlike the Linear Sprint, however, there won't be any large jumps from chord to chord. This is because there is smooth *voice-leading* from chord to chord. In other words, each note in the chord moves to the closest voice of the next chord. Because of this, the second chord of each measure ends up in *second inversion* (with the 5th on the bottom). Think of each note in the chord as a singer in a quartet and listen for a clear sound as the voices move through the pattern.

Variations:

1. Practice Linear Sprint #11 with a short, detached staccato feel. Play at a soft, consistent volume.
2. Practice Linear Sprint #11 with the hands two octaves apart.
3. Practice Linear Sprint #11 blocking each four-note 7th chord.
4. Practice Chord-Toner #11 with the chords arpeggiated instead of blocked. Play slow eighth notes starting at the lowest note and play upward through the chord. The chords will change every two beats.

Warm-Ups #1-4
Linear Sprint #12

This exercise features a two-note pattern of diatonic 3rds (using only notes found in the key), shown here in the key of B Major. Transpose to as many keys as you can.

Chord-Toner #12

Take yesterday's Chord-Toner (#11 on page 34), change the quality of the first chord of each measure to a minor 7, and you've got a widely used chord *progression* (sequence of chords) called the *ii-V*. Usually, this progression resolves to the **I** chord but for now, we're going to play **ii-V** through the cycle of 4ths. Combined with the voice-leading we learned in Chord-Toner #11, this exercise may sound familiar since it flows in a musical way. Focus on maintaining a good sound as you move through the progression.

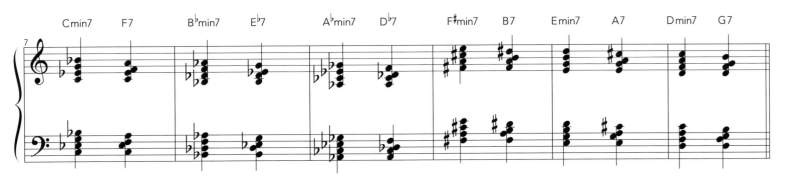

Variations:

1. Practice Linear Sprint #12 with a short, detached staccato feel. Play at a soft, consistent volume.
2. Practice Linear Sprint #12 with the hands two octaves apart.
3. Practice Linear Sprint #12 moving the two-note pattern upward chromatically instead of diatonically. Go up through the next octave and then back down.
4. Practice Chord-Toner #12 with the chords arpeggiated instead of blocked.

DAY FIFTEEN
Warm-Ups #1-4
Linear Sprint #13

30 DAY KEYBOARD WORKOUT

✓	✓	✓	✓	✓	✓	✓
✓	✓	✓	✓	✓	✓	✓
15	16	17	18	19	20	21
22	23	24	25	26	27	28
29	30					

This exercise features a two-note pattern of diatonic 4ths, shown here in the key of G♭ Major. Transpose to as many keys as you can.

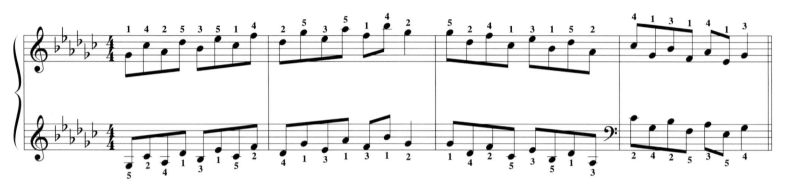

Chord-Toner #13

Today's Chord-Toner features the full ii-V-I progression. Notice that this is the first exercise where the left and right hands are playing different notes. The chords are now voiced in *open position*, which means that the notes of the chord are spaced more openly on the keyboard (spread out over more than one octave), as opposed to *close position*, where the chord tones are placed as close together as possible (usually within an octave). All the chords we've seen thus far were in close position. Continue chromatically down through the keys until you reach C again.

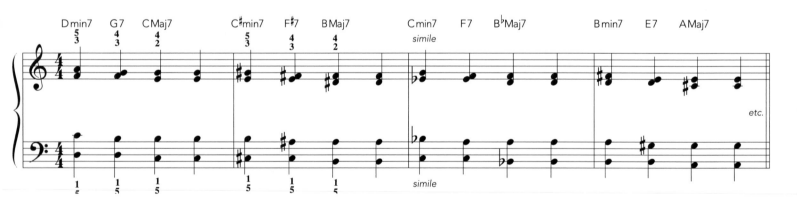

Variations:

1. Practice Linear Sprint #13 with a short, detached staccato feel. Play at a soft, consistent volume.
2. Practice Linear Sprint #13 with the hands two octaves apart.
3. Practice Linear Sprint #13 moving the two-note pattern upward chromatically instead of diatonically. Go up through the next octave and then back down.
4. Practice Chord Toner #13 with the chords arpeggiated instead of blocked.

DAY SIXTEEN
Warm-Ups #1-4
Linear Sprint #14

Play the following chromatic interval pattern as shown. This exercise works the intervals of a *minor 6th* (eight half steps) and *perfect 5th* (seven half steps). Once you are comfortable with the exercise, try going up and down two octaves.

30 DAY KEYBOARD WORKOUT						
1	2	3	4	5	6	7
8	9	10	11	12	13	14
15	16	17	18	19	20	21
22	23	24	25	26	27	28
29	30					

Chord-Toner #14

Today's exercise includes diatonic chords built with 4ths. It is shown here in the key of C Major. Start slowly and build up to a crisp quarter note rhythm. Transpose to other keys.

Variations:

1. Practice Linear Sprint #14 with a short, detached staccato feel. Play at a soft, consistent volume.
2. Practice Linear Sprint #14 with the hands two octaves apart.
3. Practice Chord-Toner #14 with the chords arpeggiated instead of blocked.
4. Play each chord from Chord-Toner #14 up and down through an octave chromatically.

30 DAY KEYBOARD WORKOUT						
✓	✓	✓	✓	✓	✓	✓
✓	✓	✓	✓	✓	✓	✓
15	16	17	18	19	20	21
22	23	24	25	26	27	28
29	30					

DAY SEVENTEEN
Warm-Ups #1-4
Linear Sprint #15

This exercise is a scale pattern similar to the Linear Sprint in Day Six (page 24). Instead of working through the major scale, however, this Linear Sprint is based on the *natural minor* scale (1-2-♭3-4-5-♭6-♭7). Once you've completed this exercise, try it in other keys. The notes and fingerings for minor scales can be found starting on page 90 of the Appendix.

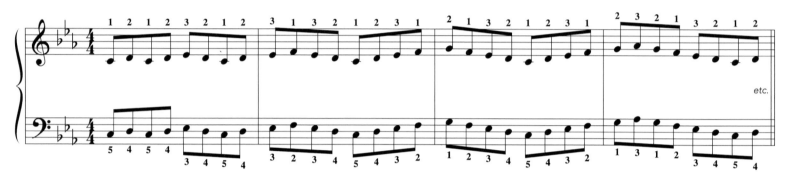

Chord-Toner #15

Here's another exercise using diatonic chords that are built with 4ths. It is shown here in the key of C Minor. Play with half notes as shown and also with quarter notes (playing each chord twice). Transpose to other keys.

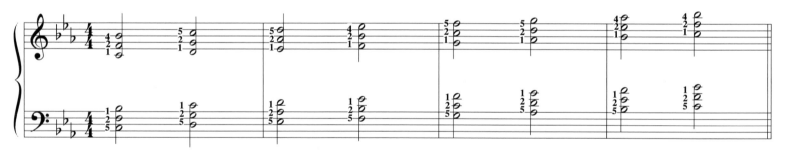

Variations:

1. Practice Linear Sprint #15 with a short, detached staccato feel. Play at a soft, consistent volume.
2. Practice Linear Sprint #15 with the hands two octaves apart.
3. Practice Chord-Toner #15 with the chords arpeggiated instead of blocked.
4. Practice playing each chord from Chord-Toner #15 up and down through an octave chromatically.

DAY EIGHTEEN
Warm-Ups #1-4
Linear Sprint #16

30 DAY KEYBOARD WORKOUT

1	2	3	4	5	6	7
8	9	10	11	12	13	14
15	16	17	18	19	20	21
22	23	24	25	26	27	28
29	30					

This exercise uses ascending and descending arpeggiated minor 7 chords. Lift your hands from the forearms right before your first note and as the hands land, keep the wrists from collapsing and let the hands "roll" through the arpeggio. Once you've played the last note of each chord, perform the same lift before starting the new one.

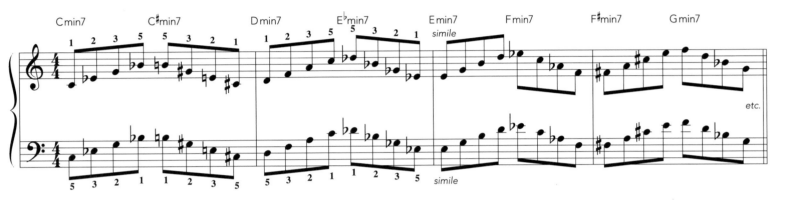

Chord-Toner #16

This Chord-Toner has a one-bar progression which moves from a very close position to a more open position. It is shown with two eighth notes per chord to build forearm strength. As usual, each chord should have a clean sound. Below, the exercise starts on C and moves to C#, D and then E♭. Continue upwards until you have played the progression in all twelve keys.

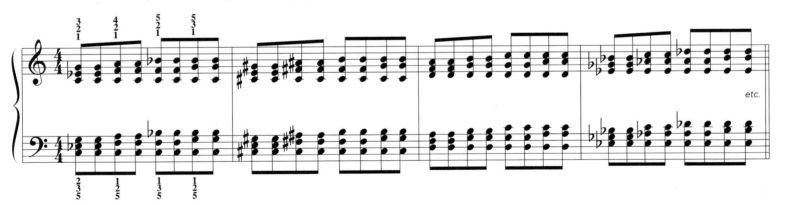

Variations:

1. Practice Linear Sprint #16 with a short, detached staccato feel. Play at a soft, consistent volume.
2. Practice Linear Sprint #16 with the hands two octaves apart.
3. Practice Linear Sprint #16 with the chords blocked.
4. Practice Chord-Toner #16 with the chords arpeggiated in sixteenth-note triplets.

DAY NINETEEN
Warm-Ups #1-4
Review

1	2	3	4	5	6	7
8	9	10	11	12	13	14
15	16	17	18	19	20	21
22	23	24	25	26	27	28
29	30					

Today is the third review day. Practice the Linear Sprints from Day Twelve (page 32) to Day Eighteen (page 39). Try all the variations listed and try some new variations of your own, such as different tempos or dynamic levels.

DAY TWENTY
Warm-Ups #1-4
Review

1	2	3	4	5	6	7
8	9	10	11	12	13	14
15	16	17	18	19	20	21
22	23	24	25	26	27	28
29	30					

Today is the fourth review day. Practice each Chord-Toner from Day Twelve (page 33) to Day Eighteen (page 39). Try playing them in all keys and with the variations. Try some new dynamic levels.

DAY TWENTY-ONE
Warm-Ups #1-4
Linear Sprint #17

1	2	3	4	5	6	7
8	9	10	11	12	13	14
15	16	17	18	19	20	21
22	23	24	25	26	27	28
29	30					

Here is a study that works with the intervals of a minor 7th (ten half steps) and major 6th (nine half steps). Play the pattern chromatically as shown. Master this exercise with the following two different playing techniques:

1) Let the hands rock from side to side as you reach for the intervals.
2) Keep the palms of your hands face down and exaggerate the lifting of the fingers.

Chord-Toner #17

Here is a chord progression based on a work by Johann Pachelbel. It is shown in the key of G Major and is composed entirely of triads. Notice how the use of inversions gives us a nice chord melody while only using a few different chords. Make sure all the notes in both hands are synchronized, and try to make the outer notes (top note of each right-hand chord and bottom note of each left-hand chord) a little louder than the inner notes.

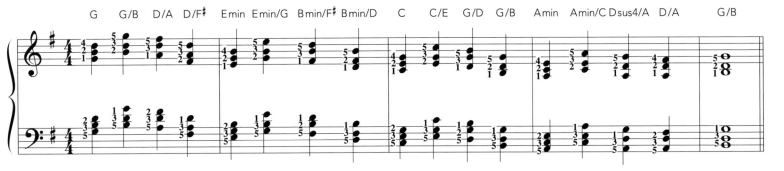

Variations:

1. Practice Linear Sprint #17 with a short, detached staccato feel. Play at both soft (*p*) and loud (*f*) dynamic levels.

2. Practice Linear Sprint #17 with the hands two octaves apart.

3. Practice Chord-Toner #17 with the chords arpeggiated. Play slow triplets starting at the lowest pitched tone and play upward through the chord.

DAY TWENTY-TWO

Warm-Ups #1-4
Linear Sprint #18

This exercise deals with an expressive device called the slur. Slurs are indicated by a phrase mark:

In this exercise, lift from the forearms and land into the first note of a slur. Think of that energy moving toward the next note and lift off the keyboard from the last note of the slur. This lifting will set you up for the next slur. Exaggerate this action for now. When playing pieces, you probably won't put this much energy into a slur with just two notes. For now, however, it's a good chops builder. Continue the sequence until you play it in all keys.

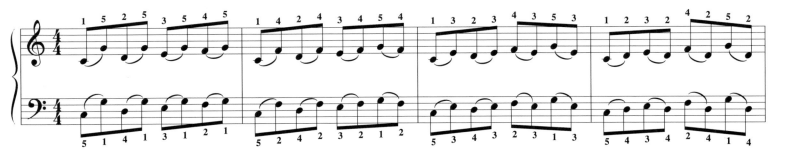

Chord-Toner #18

Here is a little etude in which the hands cross over and under each other. The dotted lines point to where each hand should move. Notice the block chords with the *marcato* markings Λ (even more attack than accents >).

The pattern is shown first in C Minor and then in F Minor. Continue through the cycle of 4ths. If necessary, refer to the scales and chords in minor keys shown starting on page 90. Keep an even tempo throughout.

Variations:

1. Practice Linear Sprint #18 with a short, detached staccato feel. Play at a soft, consistent volume.
2. Practice Linear Sprint #18 with the hands two octaves apart (without looking at the keys).
3. Practice Chord-Toner #18 at the softest level possible.

DAY TWENTY-THREE
Warm-Ups #1-4
Linear Sprint #19

30 DAY KEYBOARD WORKOUT

1	2	3	4	5	6	7
8	9	10	11	12	13	14
15	16	17	18	19	20	21
22	23	24	25	26	27	28
29	30					

In today's Linear Sprint, the pattern includes *octaves* (twelve half steps) and major 7ths (eleven half steps), which are the widest leaps to appear in the workouts so far. Master this exercise with the techniques discussed in Linear Sprint #17 (page 40). When you use finger 5 in either hand, make sure to play each key with the fingertips as opposed to leaning on the outer side of the finger. Support finger 5 by slightly curving the finger and keeping the palm firm (not too tense, though).

Chord-Toner #19

This exercise has a chord progression that may sound familiar. It is based on the ragtime piano style. Notice the left-hand movement from single note to chord. Play slowly at first, getting the left hand in position before sounding each chord. It is shown here in the key of C Major. Try other keys as well.

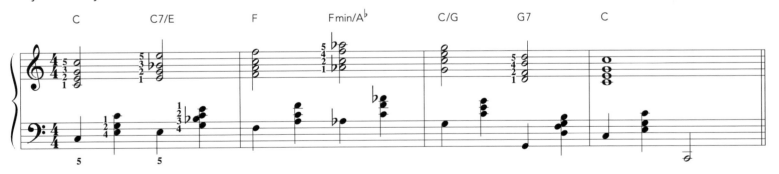

Variations:

1. Practice Linear Sprint #19 with a short, detached staccato feel. Play at both *piano* (soft) and *forte* (loud) dynamic levels.
2. Practice Linear Sprint #19 up and down two octaves.
3. Practice the right-hand part of Chord-Toner #19 with both hands.
4. Practice the left-hand part of Chord-Toner #19 with both hands.

DAY TWENTY-FOUR

Warm-Ups #1-4
Linear Sprint #20

Here is a trill study that uses three-note slurs. Use the same down-up motion introduced in Sprint #18 (page 41), keeping a legato (smooth) feel through the phrase. Make sure to lift at the end of the slur, giving a sense of "breathing" between phrases.

Chord-Toner #20

Play the chords shown below with solid timing and a smooth transition from chord to chord. It begins with another classic progression: I-vi-ii-V. This example contains some chords that are appearing for the first time in this book, so take a look at the way they are constructed. Try the entire exercise in other keys.

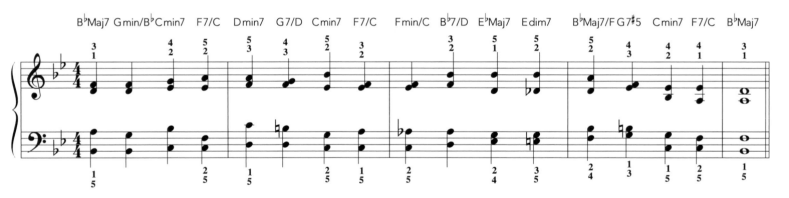

Variations:

1. Practice Linear Sprint #20 with a short, detached staccato feel. Play at both piano and forte levels.
2. Practice Linear Sprint #20 with the hands two octaves apart.
3. Practice Chord-Toner #20 playing two eighth notes on each chord. Play at a strong volume and with a nice forearm lift.

DAY TWENTY-FIVE

Warm-Ups #1-4
Linear Sprint #21

Today's Linear Sprint is a chops-building trill study. Notice the instructions in the first measure. By holding down fingers 1 and 5 in both hands, fingers 2, 3 and 4 get a great workout. Be careful not to let the hands become tense. The more you play this exercise, the sooner you will develop the finger independence and strength required for playing clean trills at various tempos and volumes.

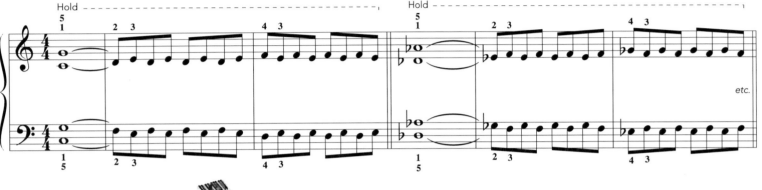

Chord-Toner #21

Now that you've given fingers 2, 3 and 4 a workout in today's Linear Sprint, try the chord pattern below. Fingers 3 and 4 in the right hand change within each chord, changing the chord quality. As with all the chord exercises, work for smooth transitions and a clear, crisp sound on each chord. Once you complete the two-measure pattern, transpose down a whole step and start again. It is shown here in the keys of F and E♭. Continue transposing the pattern down by whole step until you return to F.

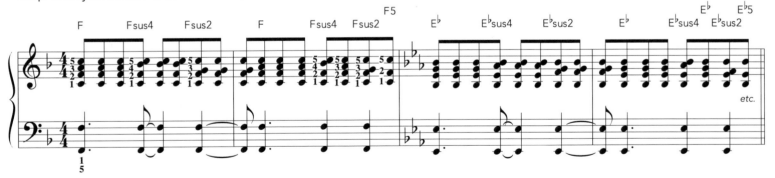

Variations:

1. Practice Linear Sprint #21 with a short, detached staccato feel (still holding down fingers 1 and 5 throughout). Play at both piano and forte levels.
2. Practice Linear Sprint #21 with the hands two octaves apart.
3. Practice Chord-Toner #21 accenting each new chord quality. For example, accent the first chord, then accent again when the chord changes to Fsus4, again at Fsus2, etc.

Warm-Ups #1-4
Linear Sprint #22

Today's Linear Sprint focuses on the *left-hand crossover*. The pattern consists of an ascending and descending arpeggio of the four basic triad qualities, with the left hand crossing over the right hand for a two-octave jump. When crossing over, keep the hand as low as possible without hitting the right hand, of course. This will help you land in time, especially at faster tempos. Remember to keep the fingertips firm each time the hand lands for a clean, balanced sound. Try this in all keys.

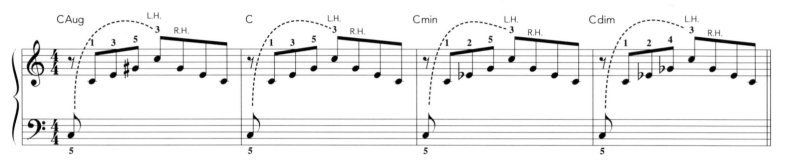

Chord-Toner #22

Here is an etude featuring right-hand 4th voicings. Starting with F7sus, the chords move up in whole steps through the first four measures. In the fifth measure, they start from F#7sus and ascend again. The chords are also given in descending order.

Variations:

1. Practice Linear Sprint #22 with a short, detached staccato feel. Play at both piano and forte levels.
2. Practice Chord-Toner #22 giving a short staccato sound to all the quarter notes.

Warm-Ups #1-4
Linear Sprint #23

At first glance, the following exercise may look more like a Chord-Toner than a Linear Sprint, but this etude is a good tremolo study, especially when brought up to a very swift tempo (remember to play slowly at first, of course). The right hand has a 1-5 *tremolo* (a rapid alternation between two notes or chords) in octaves. Because of the stretch, the hand will naturally rock back and forth. This is fine. Just remember to keep the fingers firm and don't let the hand or wrist become tense. The left hand is boogieing along with blocked 5ths and 6ths, creating a 2-1 trill pattern.

Chord-Toner #23

Here is another etude featuring 4th voicings, similar to Chord Toner #22 (page 46). This time, the left hand plays the chords and the right hand plays octaves. Although this exercise begins with a different chord, the pattern is the same as in Chord-Toner #22.

Variations:

1. Practice Linear Sprint #23 with a short, detached staccato feel. Play at both *piano* and *forte* levels.
2. Practice Chord-Toner #23 giving a short staccato sound to all the quarter notes.

DAY TWENTY-EIGHT
Warm-Ups #1-4
Linear Sprint #24

Here is another chops-builder, this time in $\frac{3}{4}$ time. Make a strong accent on the first beat of each measure. It is shown here starting on C and then D♭. Continue to move up chromatically through the remaining twelve keys.

Chord-Toner #24

This exercise uses *slash chords*, which are chords that use a bass note other than the root of the chord. Often (and in this case), this is a note not normally found in the chord. The characters to the left of the slash represent the chord. The letter to the right of the slash indicates the bass note. Putting unexpected notes under routine chords can produce some interesting sounds.

Chord-Toner #24 has right-hand triads ascending through a minor pentatonic scale (1-♭3-4-5-♭7). The left hand plays in the octave below, one note-name higher than the right-hand chord. So if the right hand plays a C triad, the left hand plays D; right hand plays a G triad, left hand plays A, etc. C/D can also be written as D11, F/G can be written as G11, etc. The two-measure pattern is show here in C, then in B. Continue down chromatically through all twelve keys.

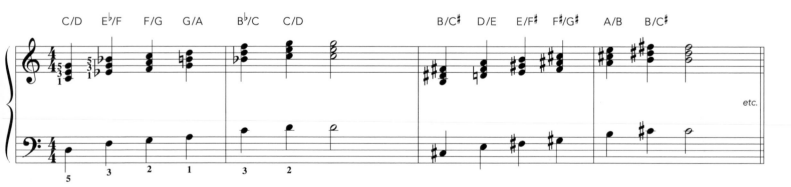

Variations:

1. Practice Linear Sprint #24 with a short, detached staccato feel. Play at both piano and forte levels.
2. Practice Chord-Toner #24 giving a short staccato sound to all the quarter notes.

DAY TWENTY-NINE
Warm-Ups #1-4
Review

Today is the fifth review day. Practice the Linear Sprints from Day Twenty-One (page 40) to Day Twenty-Eight (page 48). Try all the variations listed and try some new variations of your own, such as different tempos or dynamic levels.

DAY THIRTY
Warm-Ups #1-4
Review

Today is the sixth and final review day. Practice each Chord-Toner from Day Twenty-One (page 41) to Day Twenty-Eight (page 48). Try playing them in all keys and with the variations. Try some new dynamic levels.

End of the Proficiency Workout

Section Five
The Extended Proficiency Workout

The following Workout contains some new twists to some of the exercises you've already done, plus some new challenges. Keeping in mind all the suggestions given throughout the first Workout will give you a nice head start with these new exercises.

If you've decided to begin here instead of tackling the first Workout, welcome! You will find the Extended Proficiency Workout to be a valuable addition to your practice regimen. Remember, while the Extended Workout is designed to build chops, that is only one of the aspects of playing you need to work on as you go through it. The more you pay attention to the quality of your sound and the precision of your timing, the more you will benefit from tackling this Extended Workout. Make sure you pay attention to your fingers, hands, wrists and arms as you play. If you spot any unnecessary tension, loosen up. This essential to effective practice. Soon, careful practice will become second nature and you can have some *fun* with the Workout! Don't forget to learn the Warm-Ups on pages 10 through 13. They are an important part of the workout. Enjoy!

DAY ONE
Warm-Ups #1-4 (pages 10 - 13)
Linear Sprint #1A

30 DAY KEYBOARD WORKOUT						
✔2	3	4	5	6	7	
8	9	10	11	12	13	14
15	16	17	18	19	20	21
22	23	24	25	26	27	28
29	30					

We'll start off by playing a *chromatic scale* (a scale made entirely of half steps, also called *minor 2nds*) with both hands two octaves plus a major 3rd apart, ascending for three octaves then descending. Start with a slow, even tempo and gradually work up to a quicker tempo.

Chord-Toner #1A

This exercise has 7th chords built on each note of the E♭ Major scale. These are called the *diatonic 7th* chords. Diatonic means "of the key." We sometimes refer to this as a *harmonized scale*. Take a look at the first chord and you may notice that E♭ is found "inside" each hand's voicing. This is because each hand is playing the chord in second inversion, which means the 5th is the lowest note in the chord. Sound all the tones of each chord simultaneously. When moving from chord to chord, try to leave as little space between them as possible. Don't use the sustain pedal.

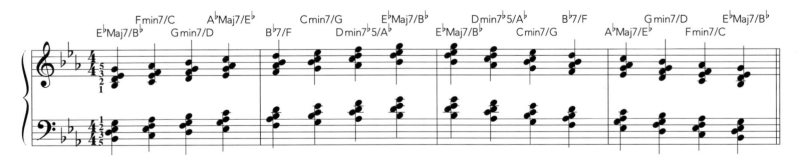

Try practicing this in all twelve keys. If necessary, refer to the Appendix starting on page 87 for key signatures. In major keys, the chord sequence is always as follows:

I	ii	iii	IV	V	vi	vii	I
Maj7	min7	min7	Maj7	Dom7	min7	min7♭5	Maj7

Variations:

1. Practice Linear Sprint #1A with the following combinations of articulation and dynamics:
    a. *legato* (smooth, connected) *piano* (soft)
    b. legato, *mezzo-forte* (medium loud)
    c. legato, *forte* (loud)
    d. legato, start piano then *crescendo* (grow louder) to highest note and *diminuendo* (grow softer) to lowest note
    e. staccato (short, detached), piano
    f. staccato, mezzo-forte
    g. staccato, forte
    h. staccato, start piano then crescendo to highest note and diminuendo to lowest note

2. Practice Chord-Toner #1A with the voicings shown below. These chords are written in *third inversion*, which means the 7th of each chord is the lowest note.

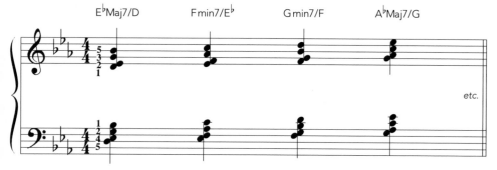

3. Play Chord-Toner #1 *arpeggiating* (breaking) the chords. In the first example, which we'll call *Ascending/Ascending*, the chords are played broken. The hands start together on the lowest note and ascend up to the highest. In the second example, both hands play the first chord broken from the lowest note to the highest and then play the second chord from the highest note to the lowest. Alternate between the two directions. We'll call this *Ascending/Descending*.

Ascending/Ascending

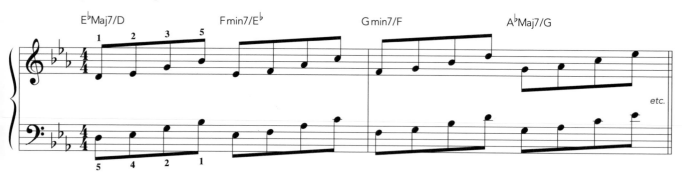

Ascending/Decending

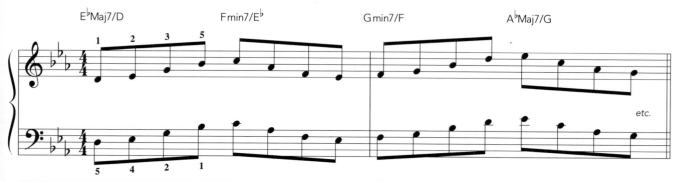

DAY TWO

Warm-Ups #1-4
Linear Sprint #2A

30 DAY KEYBOARD WORKOUT						
✔	✔	3	4	5	6	7
8	9	10	11	12	13	14
15	16	17	18	19	20	21
22	23	24	25	26	27	28
29	30					

This pattern uses the chromatic scale with the hands two-octaves-plus-a-3rd apart. Play slowly at first, paying special attention to evenness of volume. Keep that control when bringing it up to speed.

When memorizing the chromatic scale and its patterns, notice what we call the *finger 2 landings*. In the right hand, finger 2 plays C and F and in the left hand, E and B. Both hands play all other white keys with finger 1 and black keys with finger 3.

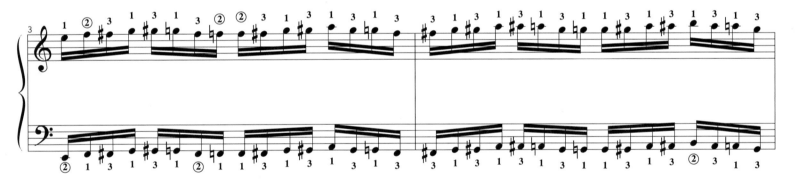

Chord-Toner #2A

Memorize the harmonized scale below. These are the diatonic 7th chords in the key of D Major. They are voiced using left-hand *shells* (the root and 7th of each chord), and the right hand plays the 3rd and 5th of each chord. Play in all keys.

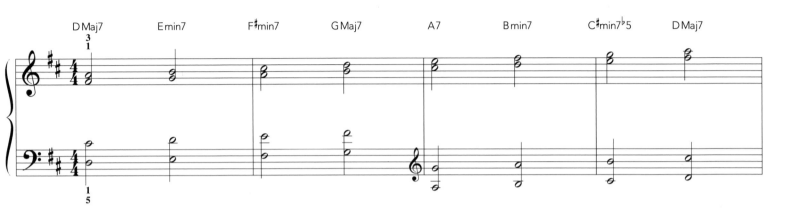

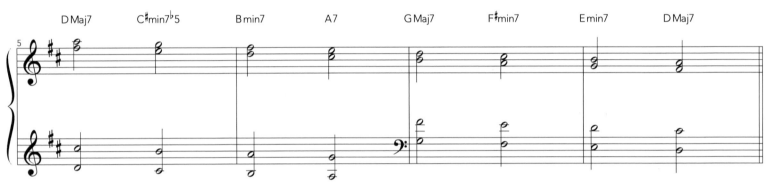

Variations:

1. Practice Linear Sprint #2A with all combinations of articulation and dynamics listed in the Variations for Day One (page 52).

2. Practice Chord-Toner #2A arpeggiating the chords Ascending/Ascending and Ascending/Descending (see Variation #3 page 52). For today's exercise, start with the left hand, moving upward through the chord and finish with the right hand. Begin descending arpeggios with the top note in the right hand as shown.

Ascending/Ascending

Ascending/Decending

DAY THREE

Warm-Ups #1-4
Linear Sprint #3A

30 DAY KEYBOARD WORKOUT						
1✓	2✓	3✓	4	5	6	7
8	9	10	11	12	13	14
15	16	17	18	19	20	21
22	23	24	25	26	27	28
29	30					

Play the following one-measure chromatic triplet pattern up through one octave. Start slowly, and be careful not to accent beats one and three of each measure. Keep the same evenness when bringing the exercise up in tempo.

Chord-Toner #3A

Memorize the following harmonized A Major scale. The left hand plays the root and 5th and the right hand plays the 3rd and 7th of each chord. Make sure all of the notes of each chord sound simultaneously, and hold each for the full two beats before moving to the next chord. Play in all keys.

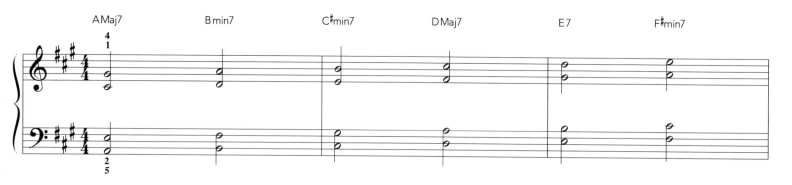

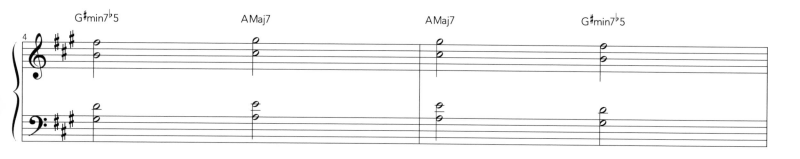

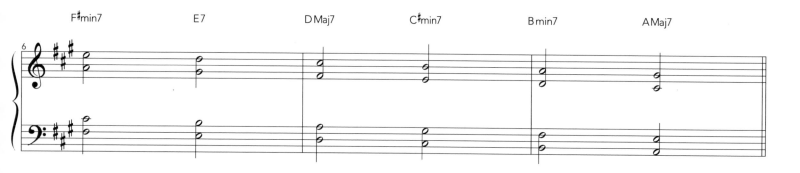

Variations:

1. Practice Linear Sprint #3A with the combinations of articulation and dynamics listed in Variation 1 for Day One (page 52).
2. Practice Chord-Toner #3A with Ascending/Ascending and Ascending/Descending arpeggios (see Variation 3, page 52).

DAY FOUR
Warm-Ups #1-4
Linear Sprint #4A

30 DAY KEYBOARD WORKOUT

1	2	3	4	5	6	7
✓	✓	✓	✓			
8	9	10	11	12	13	14
15	16	17	18	19	20	21
22	23	24	25	26	27	28
29	30					

Below is another pattern using the chromatic scale and triplets, the hands once again two-octaves-plus-a-3rd apart. Notice how often finger 3 (in both hands) crosses over each side of the thumb. Make sure your wrists stay flexible without collapsing. As usual, start slowly and go for a smooth, even sound.

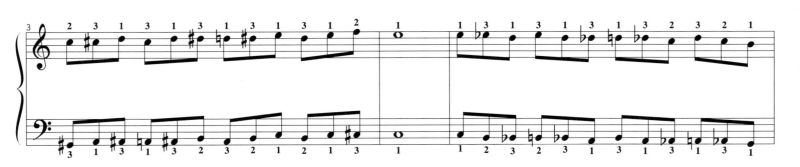

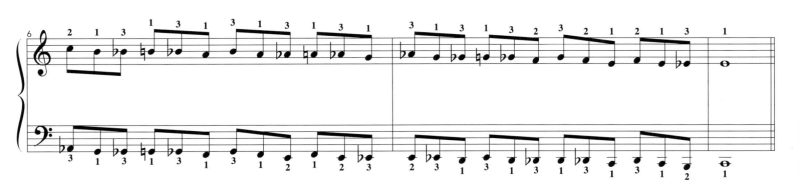

Chord-Toner #4A

This exercise makes a pattern out of the diatonic chords (harmonized scale) from Chord-Toner #1 (page 51). As with the other Chord-Toners, make sure all the notes in each chord sound simultaneously. Think ahead to the next chord shape before moving your hands. Make sure you are getting there in time. It's better to play slowly and stay in tempo than to miss a beat. Play in all keys.

Variations:

1. Practice Linear Sprint #4A with the combinations of articulation and dynamics listed in Variation 1 for Day One (page 52).
2. Practice Chord-Toner #4A with the chords in third inversion. Play in all keys.
3. Practice Chord-Toner #4A with Ascending/Ascending and Ascending/Descending arpeggios (see Variation 3, page 52). Try this in third inversion, as well.

DAY FIVE

Warm-Ups #1-4
Linear Sprint #5A

30 DAY KEYBOARD WORKOUT						
1	2	3	4	5	6	7
8	9	10	11	12	13	14
15	16	17	18	19	20	21
22	23	24	25	26	27	28
29	30					

In all the Linear Sprints so far, we've been sticking to the chromatic scale, which is made up of half steps. Today's Linear Sprint uses minor 3rds (a distance of three half steps) moving up chromatically. This exercise also includes *whole steps* (the distance of two half steps, also called *major 2nds*). Pay strict attention to the fingerings and when you're comfortable with this exercise, play it up and down through three octaves.

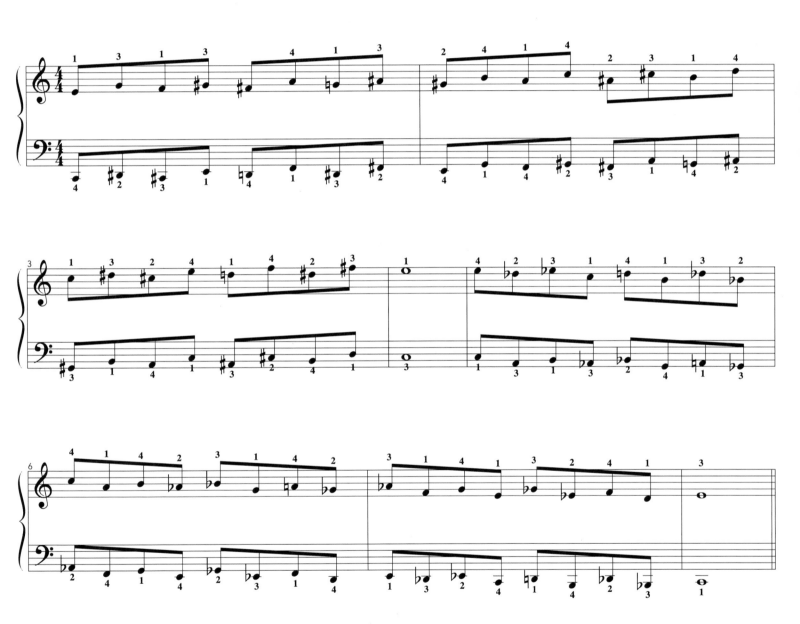

Chord-Toner #5A

This chord pattern uses the D Major diatonic 7th chords from Day Two (page 54). There's a wider jump from chord to chord, so remember to "look before you leap." Try this using the voicings from Day One (page 51) and Day Three (page 56), as well. Eventually, you will be confident about where the shapes are on the keyboard so you can play chord patterns like these without having to look at the keys. Play in all keys.

Variations:

1. Practice Linear Sprint #5A with the combinations of articulation and dynamics listed in Variation 1 for Day One (page 52).
2. Practice Chord-Toner #5A with Ascending/Ascending and Ascending/Descending arpeggios (see Variation 3 on page 52).
3. Play Chord-Toner #5A with the chords in first inversion. Play the 3rd and the 7th in the left hand and root and 5th in the right hand.

DAY SIX
Warm-Ups #1-4
Linear Sprint #6A

30 DAY KEYBOARD WORKOUT						
1	2	3	4	5	6	7
8	9	10	11	12	13	14
15	16	17	18	19	20	21
22	23	24	25	26	27	28
29	30					

Today's exercise is based on two scales: the G Major scale (in the right hand) and the E Natural Minor scale (in the left hand). Notice that both scales share the same key signature. Instead of going straight up and down the scales, however, today's Linear Sprint uses the scales in a slightly different way. It starts with the tonic (first tone), moves down one step and ascends back to the tonic. Then the scale moves down two degrees and ascends back home. Continue down four degrees, ascend, down five degrees, ascend, etc. By the end of the exercise, you'll have completed the scales. Try it in all keys. All major and natural minor scales and their fingerings can be found in the Appendix starting on page 87.

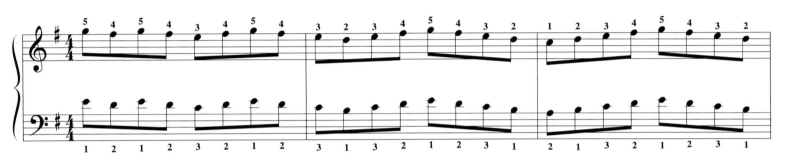

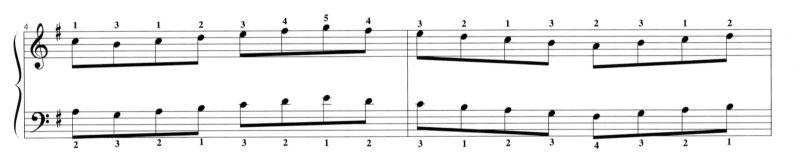

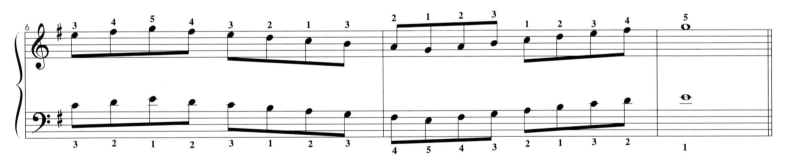

Chord-Toner #6A

This chord pattern uses the A Major chord voicings from Day Three (page 56). Play this using the voicings from Day One (page 51) and Day Two (page 54), as well. The chords move in steps as well as skips (in this case, 3rds). Play in all keys and see how you do without looking at the keyboard.

Variations:

1. Practice Linear Sprint #6A with the combinations of articulation and dynamics listed in Variation 1 for Day One (page 52).
2. Practice Linear Sprint #6A with both hands playing the major scales, one octave apart. Do the same with the natural minor scales as well.
3. Practice Chord-Toner #6A with Ascending/Ascending and Ascending/Descending arpeggios (see Variation 3, page 52).

DAY SEVEN

Warm-Ups #1-4
Linear Sprint #7A

30 DAY KEYBOARD WORKOUT

1	2	3	4	5	6	7
8	9	10	11	12	13	14
15	16	17	18	19	20	21
22	23	24	25	26	27	28
29	30					

The next three Linear Sprints are based on exercises by Charles-Louis Hanon. Unlike the originals, these patterns move within the D Major scale in the right hand and the B Natural Minor scale in the left hand. Make sure you try the variations listed on page 64, especially if you've played Hanon studies before.

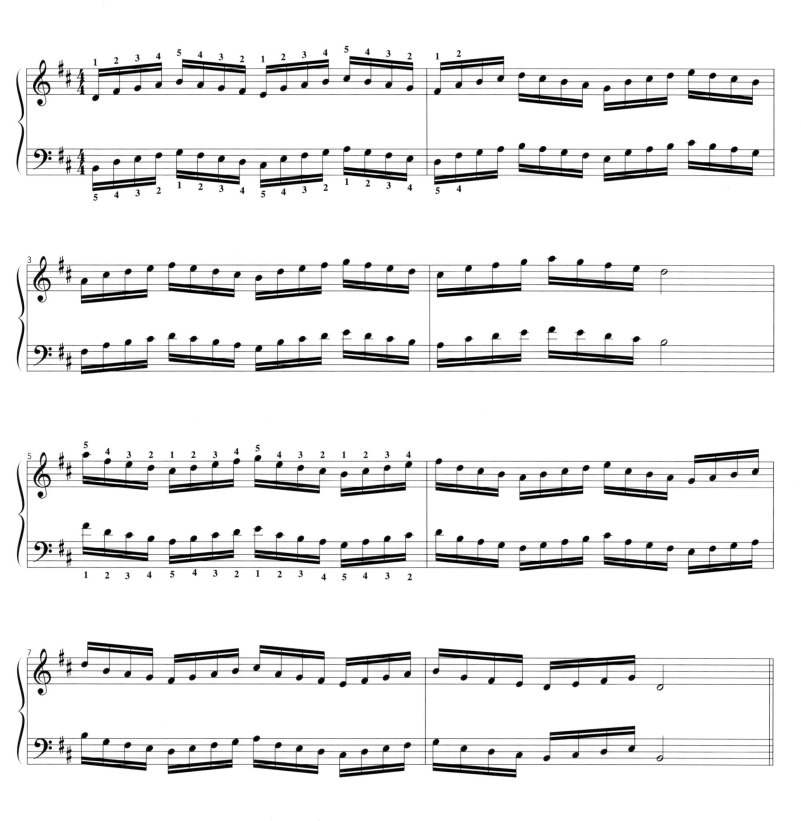

Chord-Toner #7A

This stamina-building exercise uses the diatonic 7th chords in the key of G Major. Each measure begins with repeated block chords. Each measure ends with the same voicing arpeggiated in ascending/descending order (descending/ascending from measure 9 on). Lift from the wrists when repeating the block chords at faster tempos.

Variations:

1. Practice Linear Sprint #7A with the combinations of articulation and dynamics listed in Variation 1 for Day One (page 52).
2. Play the pattern in the first measure of Linear Sprint #7A, then move it up chromatically through one octave. Then play the pattern in the ninth measure and move it down chromatically through the octave.
3. Practice Chord-Toner #7A with the chords in third inversion.

DAY EIGHT
Warm-Ups #1-4
Linear Sprint #8A

30 DAY KEYBOARD WORKOUT

✓	✓	✓	✓	✓	✓	✓
8✓	9	10	11	12	13	14
15	16	17	18	19	20	21
22	23	24	25	26	27	28
29	30					

This is the second exercise based on the works of Hanon. The pattern moves within the A Major scale in the right hand, and the F# Natural Minor in the left hand. Both scales share the key signature of three sharps. Once you are comfortable with the Linear Sprint in this key, play it in all keys.

Chord-Toner #8A

This chord pattern uses the diatonic 7th chords in the key of C with the voicings from Day Two (page 54). The chords move up a 5th, then to the octave. On the way back down, the pattern starts at the higher octave, moves down a 4th and then down to the lower octave. Play in all keys and see how you do without looking at the keyboard.

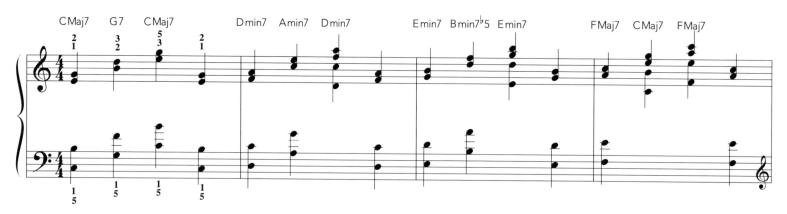

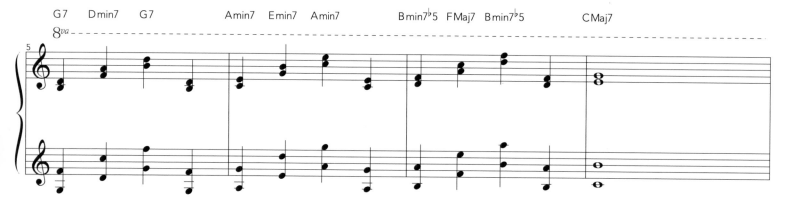

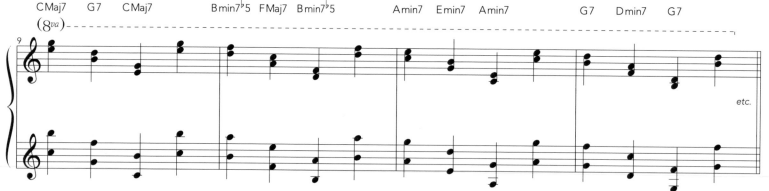

Variations:

1. Practice Linear Sprint #8A with the combinations of articulation and dynamics listed in Variation 1 for Day One (page 52).
2. Play the pattern in the first measure of Linear Sprint #8A, then move up chromatically through one octave. Then play the pattern in the ninth measure and move down in the same chromatic manner.
3. Practice Chord-Toner #8A with Ascending/Ascending and Ascending/Descending arpeggios (see variation 3 on page 52).
4. Play Chord-Toner #8A with the voicings used in Day One (page 51) and Day Three (page 56). Try it in all keys.

DAY NINE
Warm-Ups #1-4
Linear Sprint #9A

30 DAY KEYBOARD WORKOUT

1	2	3	4	5	6	7
8	9	10	11	12	13	14
15	16	17	18	19	20	21
22	23	24	25	26	27	28
29	30					

Today's Linear Sprint is the third exercise based on Hanon. It is shown here in the key of E Major in the right hand and C# Minor in the left hand. Remember to strive for an even, clear sound with no random accents. Play in all keys.

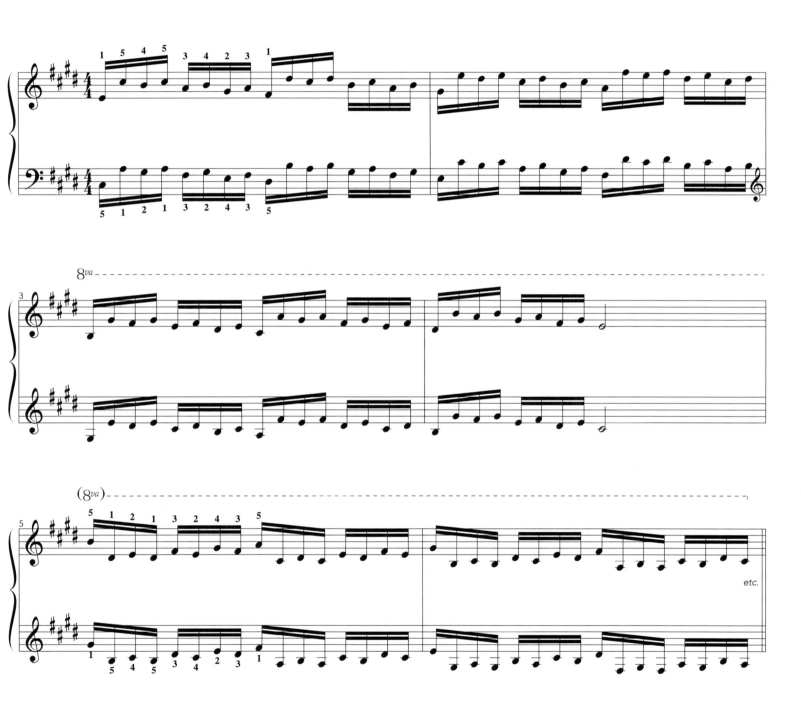

Chord-Toner #9A

This chord pattern uses the diatonic 7th chords in the key of A♭ Major with the voicings from Day Three. The pattern is as follows: I chord, the I chord up an octave, up a step to the ii chord, ii chord down an octave, up a step to the iii chord, iii chord up an octave, etc. (see page 51 to review the significance of the Roman numerals). Play in all keys.

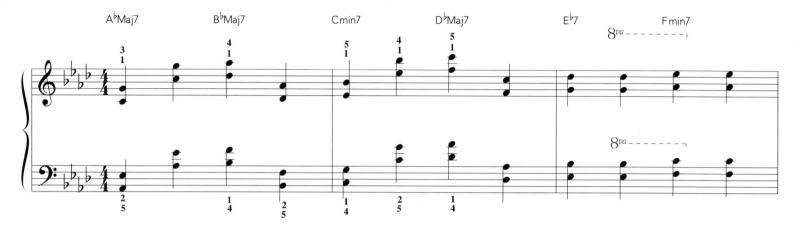

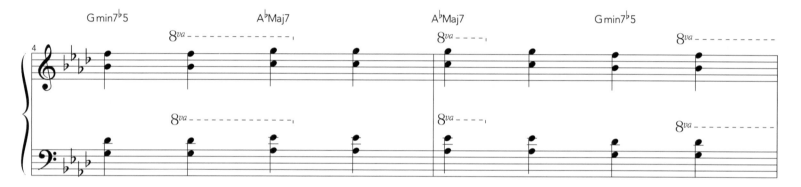

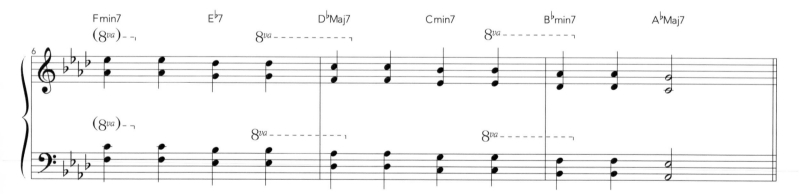

Variations:

1. Practice Linear Sprint #9A with the variations in articulation and dynamics listed in Variation 1 for Day One (page 52).
2. Play the pattern in the first measure of Linear Sprint #9A then move it up chromatically through one octave. Then play the pattern in the ninth measure and move it down chromatically through the octave.
3. Practice Chord-Toner #9A using the voicings from Day One (page 51) and Day Two (page 54).

DAY TEN
Warm-Ups #1-4
Review

Today is the first review day. Practice the nine Linear Sprints you have learned thus far. Play all the variations listed and try some new variations of your own, such as different tempos or rhythms.

DAY ELEVEN
Warm-Ups #1-4
Review

Today is the second review day. Practice the Chord-Toners from each of the first nine days. Play them in all keys and with the variations. Try some new rhythms.

DAY TWELVE
Warm-Ups #1-4
Linear Sprint #10A

Today's Linear Sprint is based on broken major triads. Start with C Major, then go up a perfect 4th (five half steps) and arpeggiate F Major, then go up a perfect 4th to B♭ and continue to move through the *cycle of 4ths* until you arrive back at C. Stay alert, since you'll be moving around the keyboard a bit more here. Stay in control.

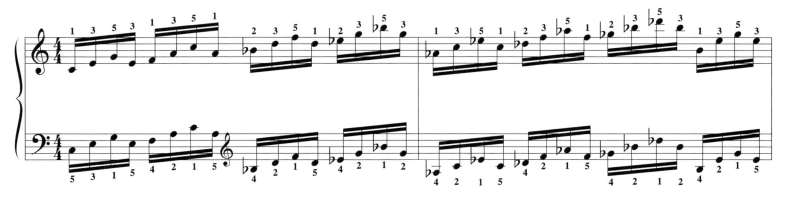

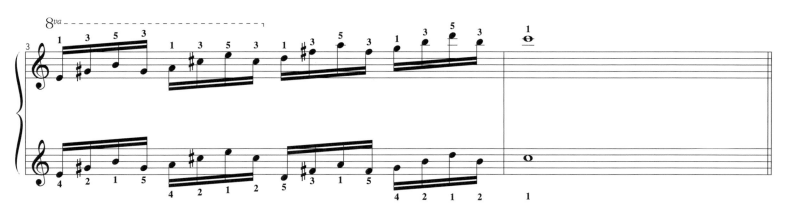

Chord-Toner #10A

Today's Chord-Toner deals with four different chord qualities. It starts with a Gmin7♭5 (G half-diminished) chord and by changing one note at a time, moves to Gmin7 (G Minor 7), G7 (G Dominant 7) and GMaj7 (G Major 7), respectively. Play the same sequence up chromatically through all twelve keys. Remember to sound all chord tones simultaneously.

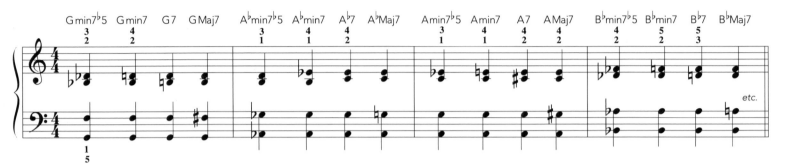

Variations:

1. Practice Linear Sprint #10A with the variations in dynamics and articulation listed in Variation 1 for Day One (page 52).
2. Practice Linear Sprint #10A with the hands two octaves apart.
3. Practice Chord-Toner #10A with Ascending/Ascending and Ascending/Descending arpeggios (see Variation 3 on page 52).
4. Play Chord-Toner #10A with the voicings from Day One (page 51) and Day Three (page 56).

DAY THIRTEEN
Warm-Ups #1-4
Linear Sprint #11A

30 DAY KEYBOARD WORKOUT						
1	2	3	4	5	6	7
8	9	10	11	12	13	14
15	16	17	18	19	20	21
22	23	24	25	26	27	28
29	30					

Here's an exercise based on a four-note pattern that consists of the root, 2nd, 3rd and 5th tone of the major scale. It moves through the cycle of 4ths. As you play the highest note in each chord, move finger 1 (right hand) and finger 5 (left hand) towards the next note to make a seamless transition to the next voicing.

Chord-Toner #11A

Today's Chord-Toner uses dominant chords moving through the cycle of 4ths. The voicings shown here add a little flavor to extend the basic 7th chord. The G in the first chord makes it an F9 and the G in the second chord makes it a B♭13. After the third bar, the pattern begins again, this time starting on C9. These voicings are often referred to as *rootless,* since the root isn't the lowest note and the voicing isn't a straight inversion.

Variations:

1. Practice Linear Sprint #11A with the variations in dynamics and articulation listed in Variation 1 for Day One (page 52).
2. Practice Linear Sprint #11A with the hands two octaves apart.
3. Practice Chord-Toner #11A with Ascending/Ascending and Ascending/Descending arpeggios (see Variation 3 on page 52). Since these chord voicings contain five notes, your arpeggios should be *quintuplets* (five notes in the time of four).

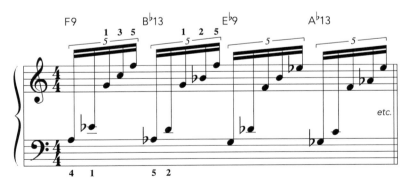

Warm-Ups #1-4
Linear Sprint #12A

30 DAY KEYBOARD WORKOUT

1	2	3	4	5	6	7
8	9	10	11	12	13	14
15	16	17	18	19	20	21
22	23	24	25	26	27	28
29	30					

This exercise features a pattern in diatonic 3rds. The right hand is in F Major, and the left hand plays the same pattern in D Minor.

Chord-Toner #12A

Take Chord-Toner #11 (page 71), change the quality of the first chord of each measure to a min9 (minor 9: 1-♭3-5-♭7-9), and you've got the famous ii-V progression. Usually, this progression resolves to the I chord but for now, we're going to play ii-V through the cycle of 4ths. These are also rootless voicings as are those in Chord Toner 11A.

Variations:

1. Practice Linear Sprint #12A with the variations in dynamics and articulation listed in Variation 1 for Day One (page 52).
2. Practice Linear Sprint #12A moving the two-note pattern upward chromatically instead of diatonically. Go up through the next octave and then back down.
3. Practice Chord-Toner #12A with Ascending/Ascending and Ascending/Descending arpeggios (see Variation 3 on page 52).

DAY FIFTEEN

Warm-Ups #1-4
Linear Sprint #13A

This exercise features diatonic 4ths. The right hand is in the key of D♭ Major and the left hand plays notes from the B♭ Natural Minor scale. Transpose this to all keys.

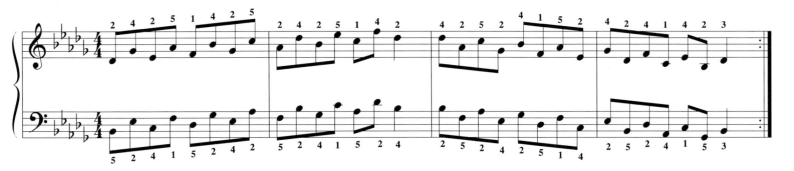

Chord-Toner #13A

Today's Chord-Toner features the full ii-V-I progression. Again, the chords are voiced using 4ths (as well as 3rds and 5ths) and are rootless. Play the progression in all keys, moving up chromatically in each measure.

Variations:

1. Play Linear Sprint #13A with the variations in dynamics and articulation listed in Variation 1 for Day One.
2. Practice Linear Sprint #13A moving the two-note pattern upward chromatically instead of diatonically. Go up through the next octave and then back down.
3. Practice Chord-Toner #13A with Ascending/Ascending and Ascending/Descending arpeggios (see Variation 3 on page 52).

30 DAY KEYBOARD WORKOUT						
1	2	3	4	5	6	7
8	9	10	11	12	13	14
15	16	17	18	19	20	21
22	23	24	25	26	27	28
29	30					

DAY SIXTEEN

Warm-Ups #1-4
Linear Sprint #14A

Play the following two-note diatonic pattern of 6ths as shown. Once you are comfortable with the exercise, try going up and down two octaves. Play in all keys.

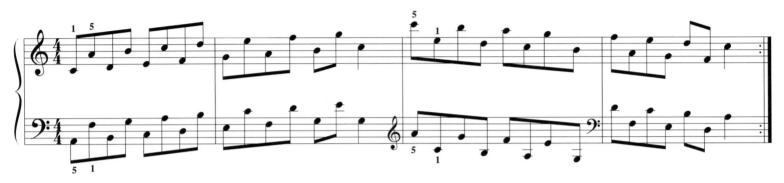

Chord-Toner #14A

Today's exercise is made up of *quartal harmonies* (chords that only use 4ths). The Maj $\frac{6}{9}$ chord (1-3-6-9) repeats and ascends chromatically through the octave. Descend back to the starting chord. Start slowly and build up to a crisp eighth-note rhythm.

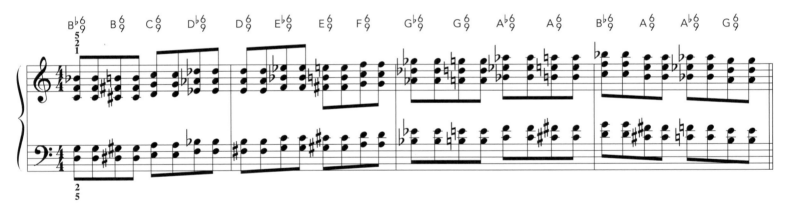

Variations:

1. Play Linear Sprint #14A with the variations in dynamics and articulation listed in Variation 1 for Day One (page 52).
2. Practice Chord-Toner #14A with Ascending/Ascending and Ascending/Descending arpeggios (see Variation 3 on page 52).

DAY SEVENTEEN
Warm-Ups #1-4
Linear Sprint #15A

This Linear Sprint uses diatonic 7ths in B♭ Major (right hand) and G Natural Minor (left hand). Once you are comfortable with the pattern, ascend and descend two octaves. Transpose to all keys.

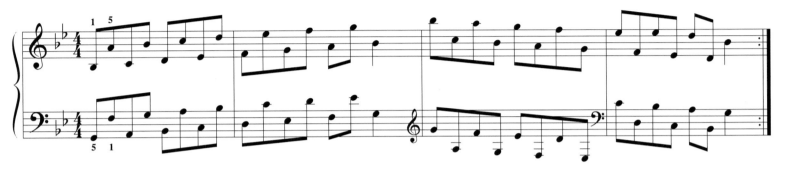

Chord-Toner #15A

Today's Chord-Toner uses a voicing for min11 chords (1-♭3-5-♭7-11), sometimes referred to as "*So What* chords." They get their nickname from a Miles Davis composition called *So What* in which these chords are prevalent. Remember to keep a steady rhythm (no matter how slow) and get a clean, crisp sound from each chord.

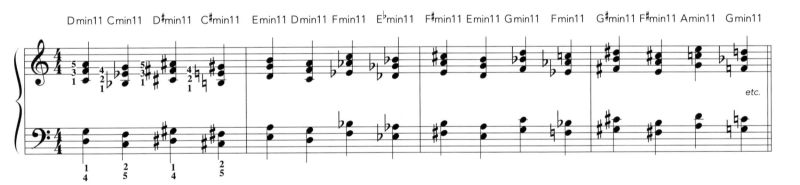

Variations:

1. Play Linear Sprint #15A with the variations in dynamics and articulation listed in Variation 1 for Day One (page 52).
2. Practice Linear Sprint #15A moving the two-note pattern upward chromatically instead of diatonically. Go up through the next octave and then back down.
3. Practice Chord-Toner #15A with Ascending/Ascending and Ascending/Descending arpeggios (see Variation 3 on page 52).

DAY EIGHTEEN
Warm-Ups #1-4
Linear Sprint #16A

In this exercise, the right hand plays a pattern of arpeggiated major triads with the octave added. The left hand is playing a pattern of octaves. Once you get the hang of it, try to master the exercise without looking at the keys. This will help develop the ability to "feel" two common shapes at the keyboard: octaves and major triads.

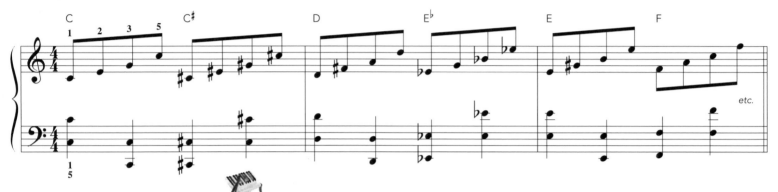

Chord-Toner #16A

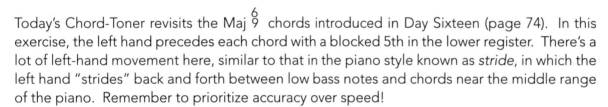

Today's Chord-Toner revisits the Maj $\frac{6}{9}$ chords introduced in Day Sixteen (page 74). In this exercise, the left hand precedes each chord with a blocked 5th in the lower register. There's a lot of left-hand movement here, similar to that in the piano style known as *stride*, in which the left hand "strides" back and forth between low bass notes and chords near the middle range of the piano. Remember to prioritize accuracy over speed!

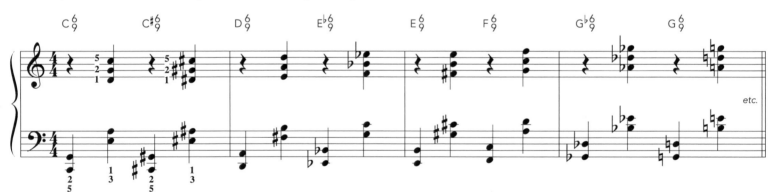

Variations:

1. Play Linear Sprint #16A with the variations in dynamics and articulation listed in Variation 1 for Day One (page 52).
2. Practice Chord-Toner #16A with Ascending/Ascending and Ascending/Descending arpeggios (see Variation 3 on page 52). Start with the left-hand blocked 5th as shown, and arpeggiate the two-hand voicing.

DAY NINETEEN
Warm-Ups #1-4
Review

30 DAY KEYBOARD WORKOUT						
1✓	2✓	3✓	4✓	5✓	6✓	
8✓	9✓	10✓	11✓	12✓	13✓	14✓
15✓	16✓	17✓	18✓	19✓	20	21
22	23	24	25	26	27	28
29	30					

Today is the third review day. Practice the Linear Sprints from Day Twelve (page 69) to Day Eighteen (page 76). Try all the variations listed and try some new variations of your own, such as different tempos or rhythms.

DAY TWENTY
Warm-Ups #1-4
Review

30 DAY KEYBOARD WORKOUT						
1✓	2✓	3✓	4✓	5✓	6✓	
8✓	9✓	10✓	11✓	12✓	13✓	14✓
15✓	16✓	17✓	18✓	19✓	20✓	21
22	23	24	25	26	27	28
29	30					

Today is the fourth review day. Practice each Chord-Toner from Day Twelve (page 70) to Day Eighteen (page 76). Try playing them in all keys and with the variations. Try some new tempos and rhythms.

DAY TWENTY-ONE
Warm-Ups #1-4
Linear Sprint #17A

30 DAY KEYBOARD WORKOUT						
1✓	2✓	3✓	4✓	5✓	6✓	
8✓	9✓	10✓	11✓	12✓	13✓	14✓
15✓	16✓	17✓	18✓	19✓	20✓	21✓
22	23	24	25	26	27	28
29	30					

Here is a study that works with all the intervals from the half step through to the octave. Play the pattern ascending and descending chromatically. Master this exercise with two different playing techniques:

1) Let the hands rock from side to side as you reach for the interval.
2) Keep the palms of your hands face down and exaggerate the lifting of the fingers.

Chord-Toner #17A

Here is a chord progression based on a work by Carl Czerny. It is shown in the key of G Major (starting on the **IV** chord, C Major) and is composed mainly of triads. Notice how the use of inversions creates a nice chord melody while only using a few different chords. Make sure all the notes in both hands are struck simultaneously, and try to make the outer notes (top note of each right-hand chord and bottom note of each left-hand chord) a little louder than the inner notes.

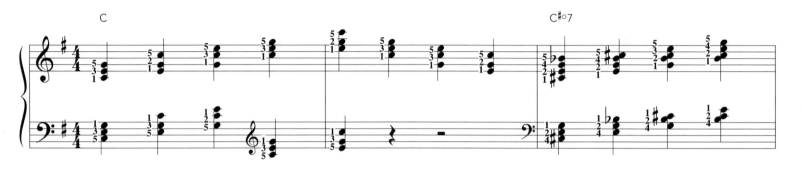

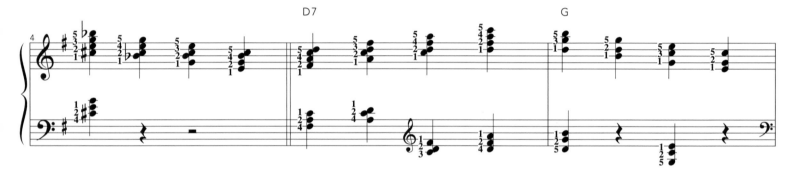

Variations:

1. Play Linear Sprint #17 with the variations in dynamics and articulation listed in Variation 1 for Day One (page 52).
2. Practice Linear Sprint #17 with the hands two octaves apart.
3. Practice Chord-Toner #17 with the chords broken. Play slow triplets starting at the lowest pitched tone and play upward through the chord.

DAY TWENTY-TWO

Warm-Ups #1-4
Linear Sprint #18A

This exercise deals with repeating notes and slurs. Make sure that both hands are playing the correct fingerings for the repeating notes. Lift from the forearms and land into the first note of a slur. Think of that energy as moving toward the next note and lift off the keyboard after the last note of the slur. This lifting will set you up for the next slur. Exaggerate this action for now. When playing pieces, you probably won't put this much energy into a slur with just two notes. For now, however, it's a good chops builder. Continue the four-bar sequence up through one octave. Play in all keys.

Chord-Toner #18A

Here is a little etude in which the hands cross over and under each other. The dotted lines point to where each hand should move. Each measure contains four different chord qualities. Play this pattern through the cycle of 4ths as shown. Keep an even tempo throughout.

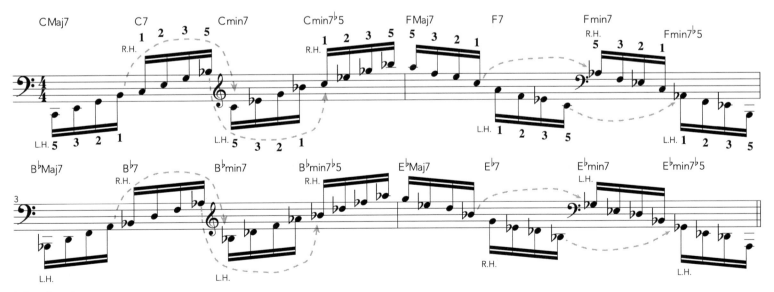

Variations:

1. Play Linear Sprint #18 with the variations in dynamics and articulation listed in Variation 1 for Day One (page 52).
2. Practice Chord-Toner #18 with the chords blocked.

DAY TWENTY-THREE

Warm-Ups #1-4
Linear Sprint #19A

In today's Linear Sprint, the right hand plays octaves in descending (and later ascending) perfect 4ths. The left hand also plays octaves on beats 1 and 3 of each measure. Keep the wrists from becoming tense as you play.

Chord-Toner #19A

Here is another stride exercise. This time, the left hand jumps from a blocked 5th to join the right hand in a dominant 9 chord (1-3-5-♭7-9). The exercise moves in the cycle of 4ths. The pattern descends. If the chords start to sound too muddy as you progress, try starting in a higher octave.

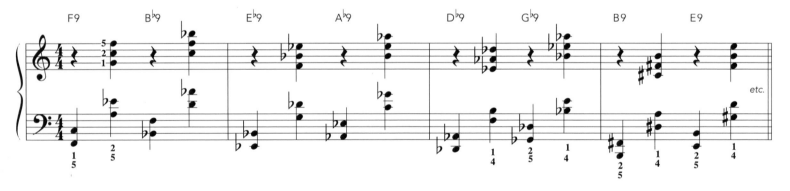

Variations:

1. Play Linear Sprint #19A with the variations in dynamics and articulation listed in Variation 1 for Day One (page 52).
2. Practice Chord-Toner #19A with Ascending/Ascending and Ascending/Descending arpeggios (see Variation 3 on page 52). Start with the left-hand blocked 5th as shown, and arpeggiate the two-hand voicing.

Warm-Ups #1-4
Linear Sprint #20A

Here is a trill study that uses three-note slurs. Use the same down-up motion introduced in Linear Sprint #18 (page 79), keeping a legato (smooth) feel through the phrase. Make sure to lift at the end of the slur, giving a sense of "breathing" between phrases. Play in all keys.

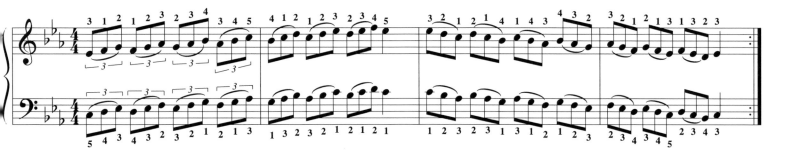

Chord-Toner #20A

Play the chords shown below with solid timing and a smooth transition from chord to chord. It is based on the first eight bars of a progression commonly associated with the Gershwin song, *I Got Rhythm*. They are often referred to as *"Rhythm Changes."* If you can, try the exercise in all keys. Some of the notes have been altered from the key signature, so keep these alterations in mind as you transpose.

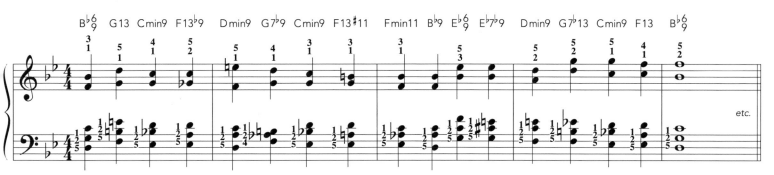

Variations:

1. Play Linear Sprint #20A with the variations in dynamics and articulation listed in Variation 1 for Day One (page 52).
2. Practice Chord-Toner #20A with Ascending/Ascending and Ascending/Descending arpeggios (see Variation 3 on page 52).

DAY TWENTY-FIVE

Warm-Ups #1-4
Linear Sprint #21A

Today's Linear Sprint is a chops-building trill study. Notice that both hands hold down finger 1 while the other fingers play the trills. Be careful not to let the hands become tense. The more you play this exercise, the sooner you will develop the finger independence and strength required for playing clean trills at various tempos and volumes. Play in all keys.

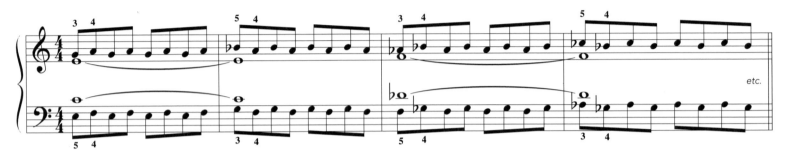

Chord-Toner #21A

Today's Chord-Toner requires a cool, two-fisted attack so don't be shy. Let loose! Shown here are the I, IV and V chords in the key of A. Try other keys, as well. Keep the eighth-note pulse strong throughout.

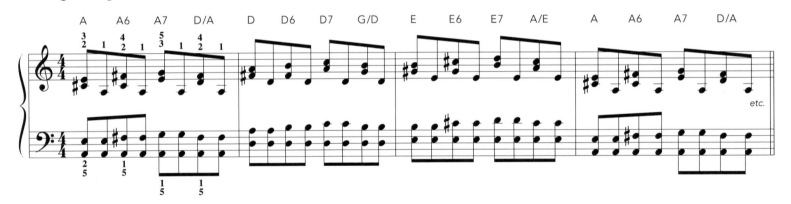

Variations:

1. Play Linear Sprint #21 with the variations in dynamics and articulation listed in Variation 1 for Day One (page 52).
2. Practice Chord-Toner #21 with Ascending/Ascending and Ascending/Descending arpeggios (see Variation 3 on page 52.
3. Practice Chord-Toner #21 giving an accent to each new chord quality. For example, accent the first chord, then accent again when the chord changes to A6, again at the A7, etc.

DAY TWENTY-SIX
Warm-Ups #1-4
Linear Sprint #22A

Today's Linear Sprint focuses on the *left-hand crossover*. The pattern consists of an ascending and descending arpeggio of the four basic triad qualities (augmented, major, minor and diminished), with the left hand crossing over the right hand for a two-octave jump. When crossing over, keep the hand as low as possible without hitting the right hand, of course. This will help you land in time, especially at faster tempos. Remember to keep the fingertips firm each time the hand lands for a clean, balanced sound.

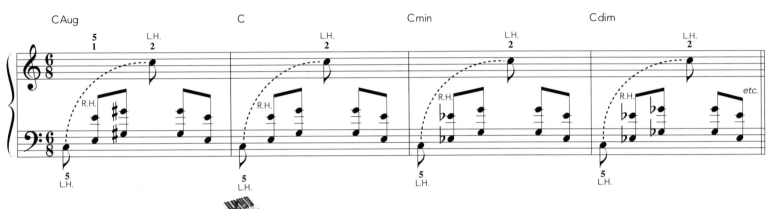

Chord-Toner #22A

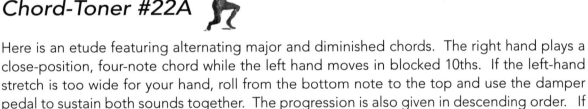

Here is an etude featuring alternating major and diminished chords. The right hand plays a close-position, four-note chord while the left hand moves in blocked 10ths. If the left-hand stretch is too wide for your hand, roll from the bottom note to the top and use the damper pedal to sustain both sounds together. The progression is also given in descending order. If you can, play this in all keys, observing the pitch alterations.

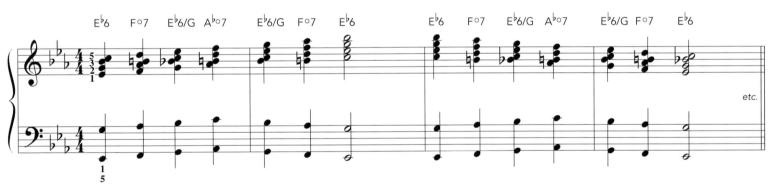

Variations:

1. Play Linear Sprint #22A with the variations in dynamics and articulation listed in Variation 1 for Day One (page 52).
2. Practice Chord-Toner #22A with Ascending/Ascending and Ascending/Descending arpeggios (see Variation 3 on page 52).

DAY TWENTY-SEVEN

Warm-Ups #1-4
Linear Sprint #23A

Today's Linear Sprint helps build stamina in two areas: 1) the left hand plays a bass boogie riff that can be quite ferocious at up-tempos; 2) the right hand has an octave trill that lasts as long as you can stand it and then some. The object here is to keep this riff going as long as you can at a decent tempo and with a quality sound.

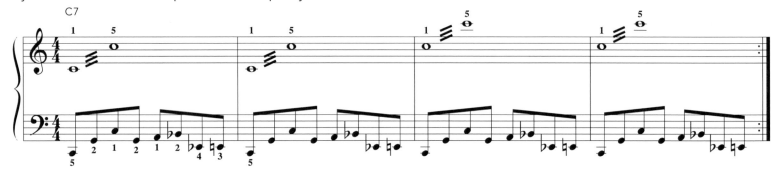

Chord-Toner #23A

Here is an etude featuring alternating minor and diminished chords. The right hand plays a close-position, four-note chord while the left hand moves in blocked 10ths. If the left-hand stretch is too wide for your hand, roll from the bottom note to the top and use the damper pedal to sustain both sounds together. The progression is also given in descending order. If you can, play this in all keys, observing the pitch alterations.

Variations:

1. Play Linear Sprint #23 with the variations in dynamics and articulation listed in Variation 1 for Day One (page 52).
2. Practice Chord-Toner #23 with Ascending/Ascending and Ascending/Descending arpeggios (see Variation 3 on page 52).

DAY TWENTY-EIGHT

Warm-Ups #1-4
Linear Sprint #24A

In some of the previous exercises, the crossover was used to play a line across the span of several octaves. In today's Linear Sprint, the right hand gets a workout on playing rapidly through four octaves on its own. The left holds down an octave trill while the right hand plays a pattern from the minor scale. Play in all keys.

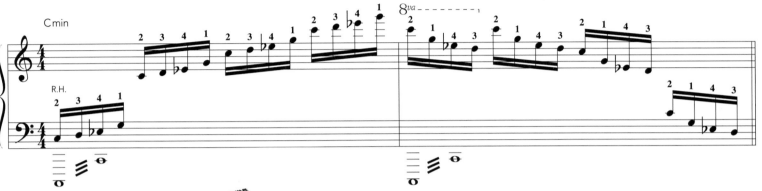

Chord-Toner #24A

The final Chord-Toner is an *etude* (study) that covers many of the chords we've seen in this book so far, with a few added surprises. It's shown here in the key of F Major. Once you've mastered it (it need not be too fast), try playing the entire etude in other keys. Most importantly, keep a steady rhythm and a clean sound.

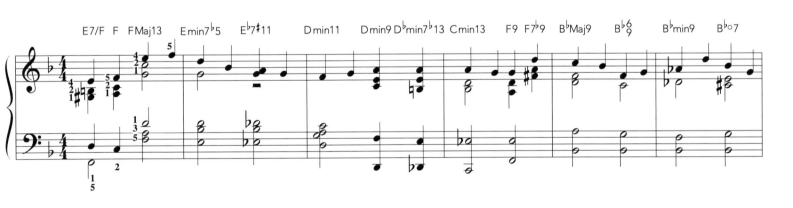

DAY TWENTY-NINE
Warm-Ups #1-4
Review

Today is the fifth review day. Practice the Linear Sprints from Day Twenty-One (page 77) to Day Twenty-Eight (page 85). Try all the variations listed and try some new variations of your own, such as different tempos and rhythms. Then you will have completed all the Linear Sprints of the Extended Proficiency Workout. Congratulations!

DAY THIRTY
Warm-Ups #1-4
Review

Today is the sixth and final review day. Now practice each Chord-Toner from Day Twenty-One (page 78) to Day Twenty-Eight (page 85). Try playing them in all keys and with the variations. Try some different tempos and rhythms. You will then have completed all the Chord-Toners of the Extended Proficiency Workout. Congratulations!

End of the Extended Proficiency Workout

Appendix

Scales and Chords

This section contains the notes and fingerings for scales and chords. Next to each scale you will find the major triad for that key shown in root position, first inversion, second inversion and finally, root position one octave higher. The twelve natural minor scales and chords are then shown in the same manner, followed by the harmonic and melodic minor scales. Notice that for each scale, finger 4 is circled whenever it is used. Knowing the *finger 4 landings* for each scale will help you memorize the fingerings.

The Twelve Major Scales and Triads

E Major

B Major

G♭ (or F♯) Major

D♭ (or C♯) Major

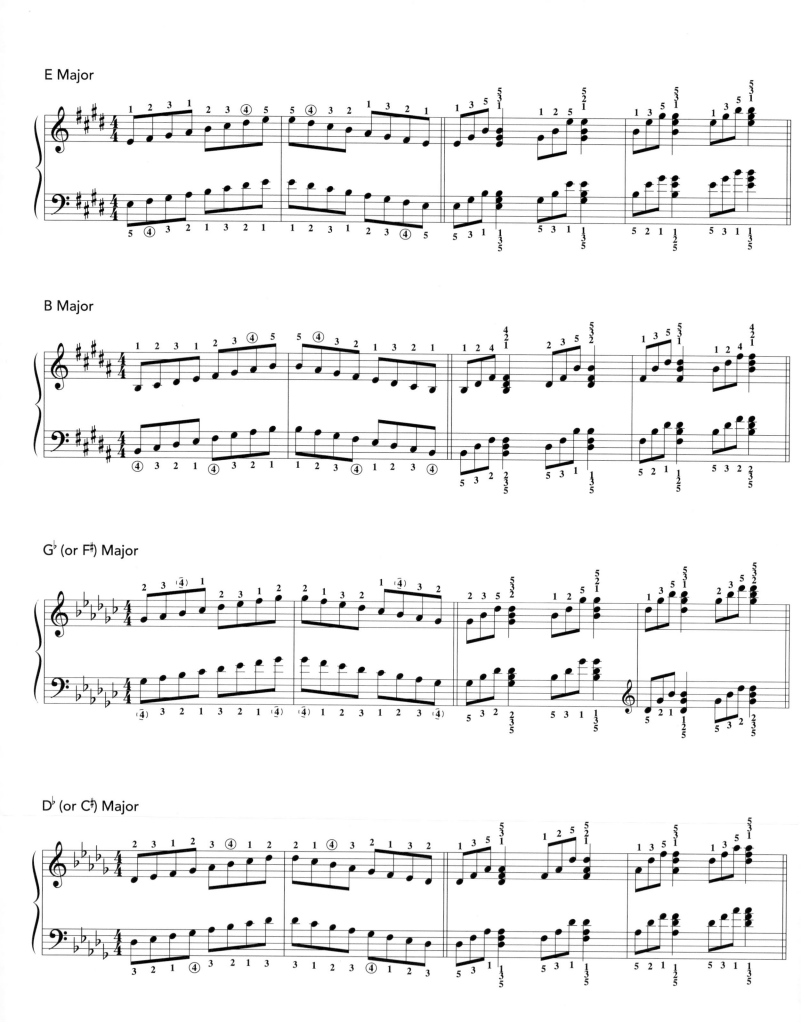

A♭ Major

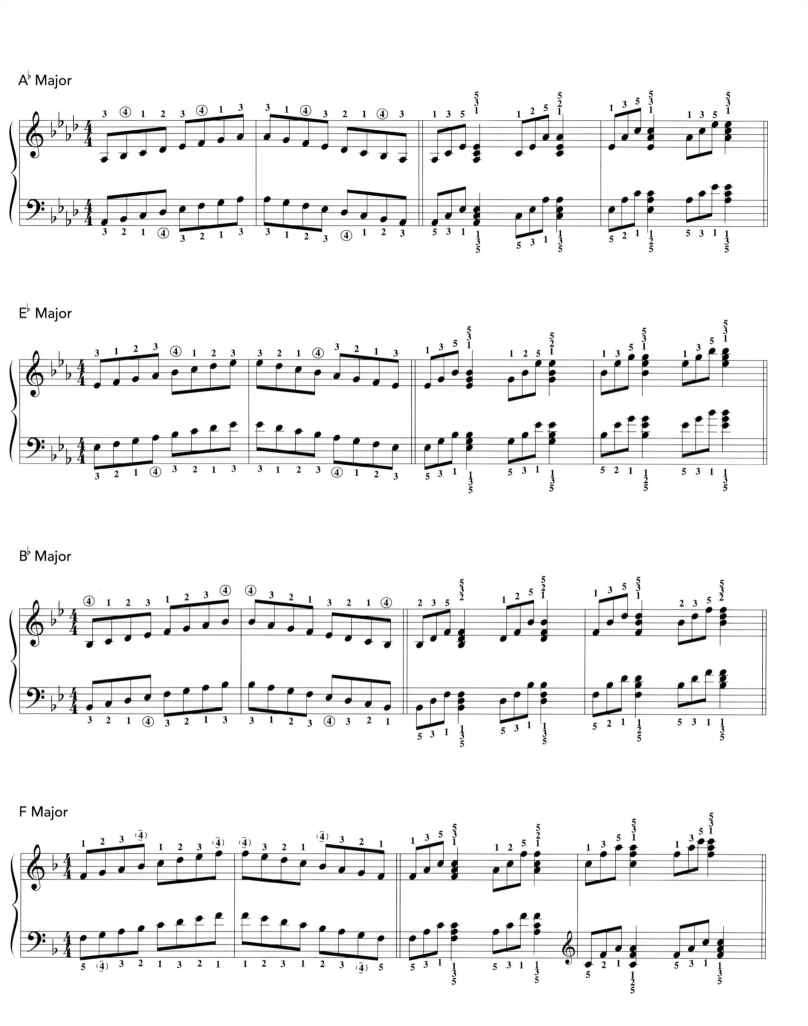

E♭ Major

B♭ Major

F Major

The Twelve Natural Minor Scales and Chords

C Natural Minor

G Natural Minor

D Natural Minor

A Natural Minor

E Natural Minor

B Natural Minor

G♭ (or F♯) Natural Minor

D♭ (or C♯) Natural Minor

A♭ (or G♯) Natural Minor

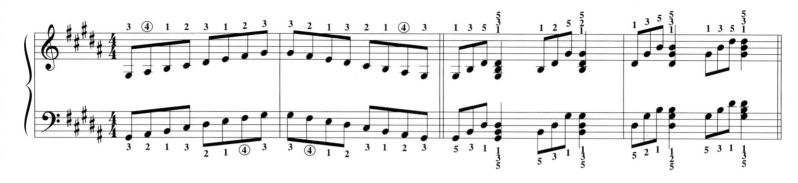

E♭ Natural Minor

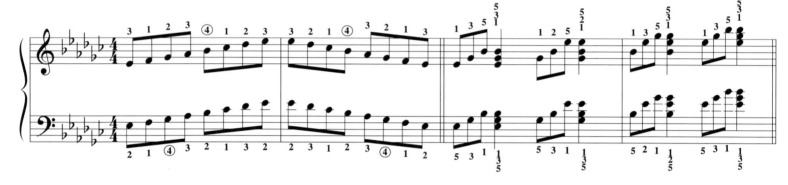

B♭ Natural Minor

F Natural Minor

The Twelve Harmonic Minor and Melodic Minor Scales

C Minor

Harmonic Minor   Melodic Minor

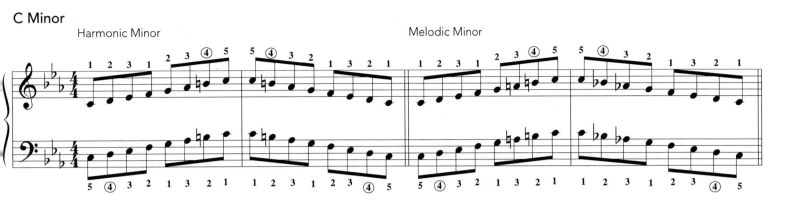

G Minor

Harmonic Minor   Melodic Minor

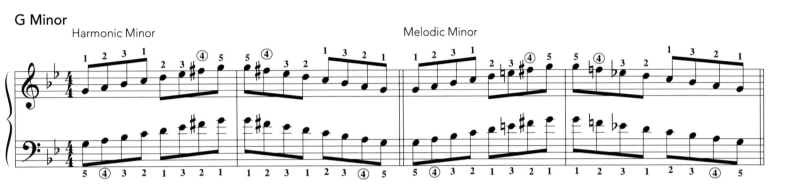

D Minor

Harmonic Minor   Melodic Minor

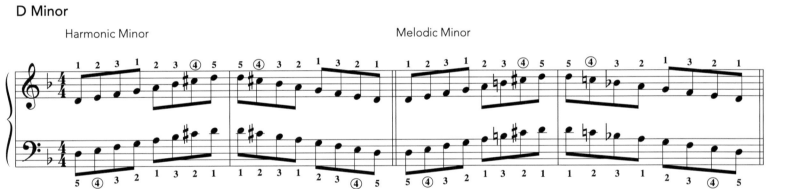

A Minor

Harmonic Minor   Melodic Minor

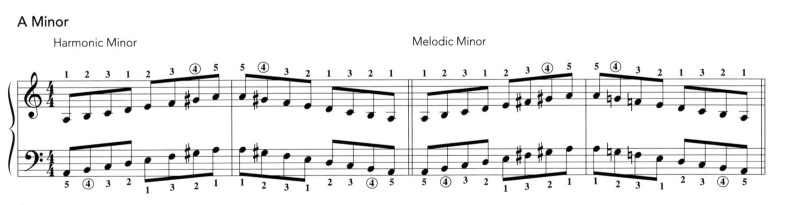

E Minor

Harmonic Minor   Melodic Minor

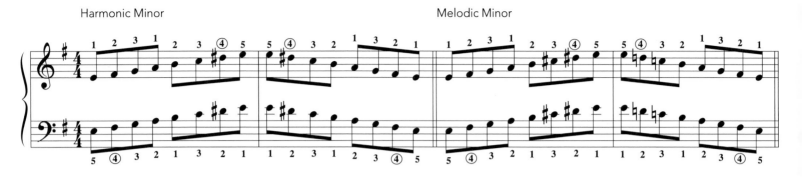

B Minor

Harmonic Minor   Melodic Minor

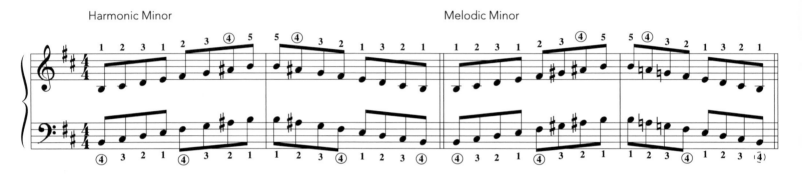

F♯ (or G♭) Minor

Harmonic Minor   Melodic Minor

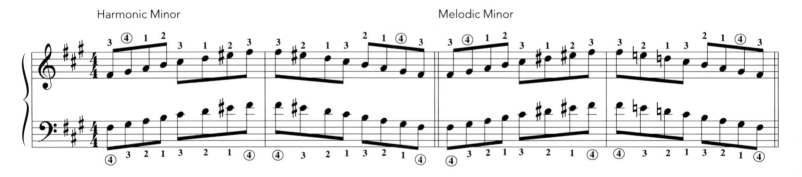

C♯ (or D♭) Minor

Harmonic Minor   Melodic Minor

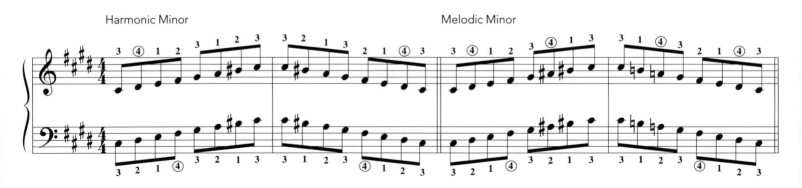

A♭ (or G♯) Minor

Harmonic Minor   Melodic Minor

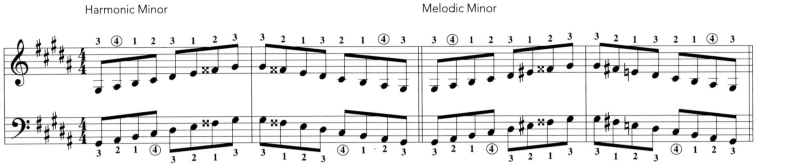

E♭ Minor

Harmonic Minor   Melodic Minor

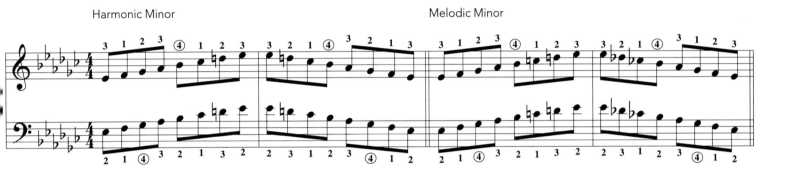

B♭ Minor

Harmonic Minor   Melodic Minor

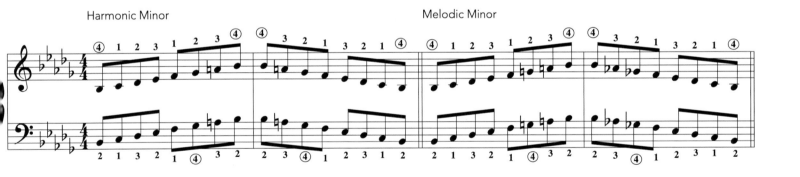

F Minor

Harmonic Minor   Melodic Minor

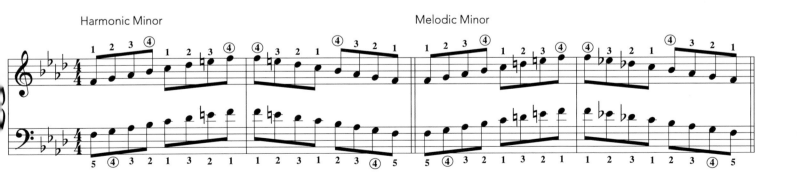